NAUTOR'S SWAN

SWAN
IS PASSION

Foreword

Leonardo Ferragamo

The 40th Anniversary of Nautor's Swan has been a tremendous source
of fulfilment and pride for us all. The anniversary has truly been a reward
for the enormous energy and hard work that has been dedicated to the company
over the last few years.

From the outset, the Swan name has been synonymous with the qualities
of elegance, enduring reliability, and lines which seem to challenge the laws
of time. In short, Swan means yachts of the highest possible quality.

Our purpose has been to uphold the treasure of this heritage, and to maintain
its legacy for the future. I remain fascinated by the company's culture,
mission and philosophy, and feel responsible for ensuring its future.

I wish to take this opportunity to thank sincerely all those who have built
this tradition, day by day.

Firstly, to all the extremely talented craftsmen: the boat builders and technicians,
who utilise their immense skills, pride and passion to make Swan unique
in the world.

Next, the management teams and all those who represent Swan around
the world, with such dedication and conviction.

Finally, my special thanks go to all Swan owners who have generously shared
with us their wisdom and opinions, who have inspired us and who have backed
Nautor's Swan over four decades. You have made Nautor's Swan what it is today!
I echo your passion for Swan with my own, because that is what Swan is: a true passion.
I dedicate this book to you all.

Introduction

Decio Giulio Riccardo Carugati

The book communicates Nautor excellence in more than one voice, bringing
the passion of Nautor's Swan to life through magical descriptions of company
tradition and its innovative approach.

Fast, reliable and safe, Swans are built for sailing, for living and experiencing
the sea. They were brought to life through the passion of those who implement
the design and those who enjoy its fruits: "Just posit a ship as a dwelling
for man," notes Roland Barthes in *Mythologies*, "and man will immediately
organise the enjoyment of a round, smooth universe of which on the other hand
a whole nautical moral makes him the god and at once the lord and master."
A special passion for "a round, smooth universe" may be recognised in the
actions of founder Pekka Koskenkylä and current main shareholder of Nautor's
Swan, Leonardo Ferragamo, but even more in the number of owners worldwide
who favour the Finnish yard's splendid vessels.

The book highlights the priorities and the values of Nautor's Swan, that are
emphasised through the contributions by Roberto Franzoni, Maria Sebregondi
and myself. Stories that complement other.

I would like to thank Kjell Vestö, Kristian Kjellman, Ulf Finnäs, Tom Blomgren,
Eva-Stina Kjellman and Lars Ström for the precious information they provided
during interviews in Finland; Paola Ciribilli, Alessandro Loni Coppedè,
Francesca Cardini and Emma Festa for the identification and analysis
of the milestones in Nautor's Swan's evolution. A shared passion cancels
out the geographical distances separating the people mentioned.

My thanks also go to Dario Tagliabue, who is in charge of graphic design,
to Anna Piccarreta, Chiara Fasoli, Virginia Ponciroli, Simona Oreglia,
Giancarlo Berti, and in the persons of Stefano Peccatori and Luciano Mornacchi,
to the whole Electa staff.

ClubSwan

"Beautiful boats lead to the creation of other beautiful boats …
Beauty is an ineffable value that should be smuggled in secret, unbeknownst
to the user. If it is manifested beforehand, all is lost. A bit like love."

(Oscar Wilde, quoted in Carlo Sciarrelli, *The Yacht*, Milan 1970)

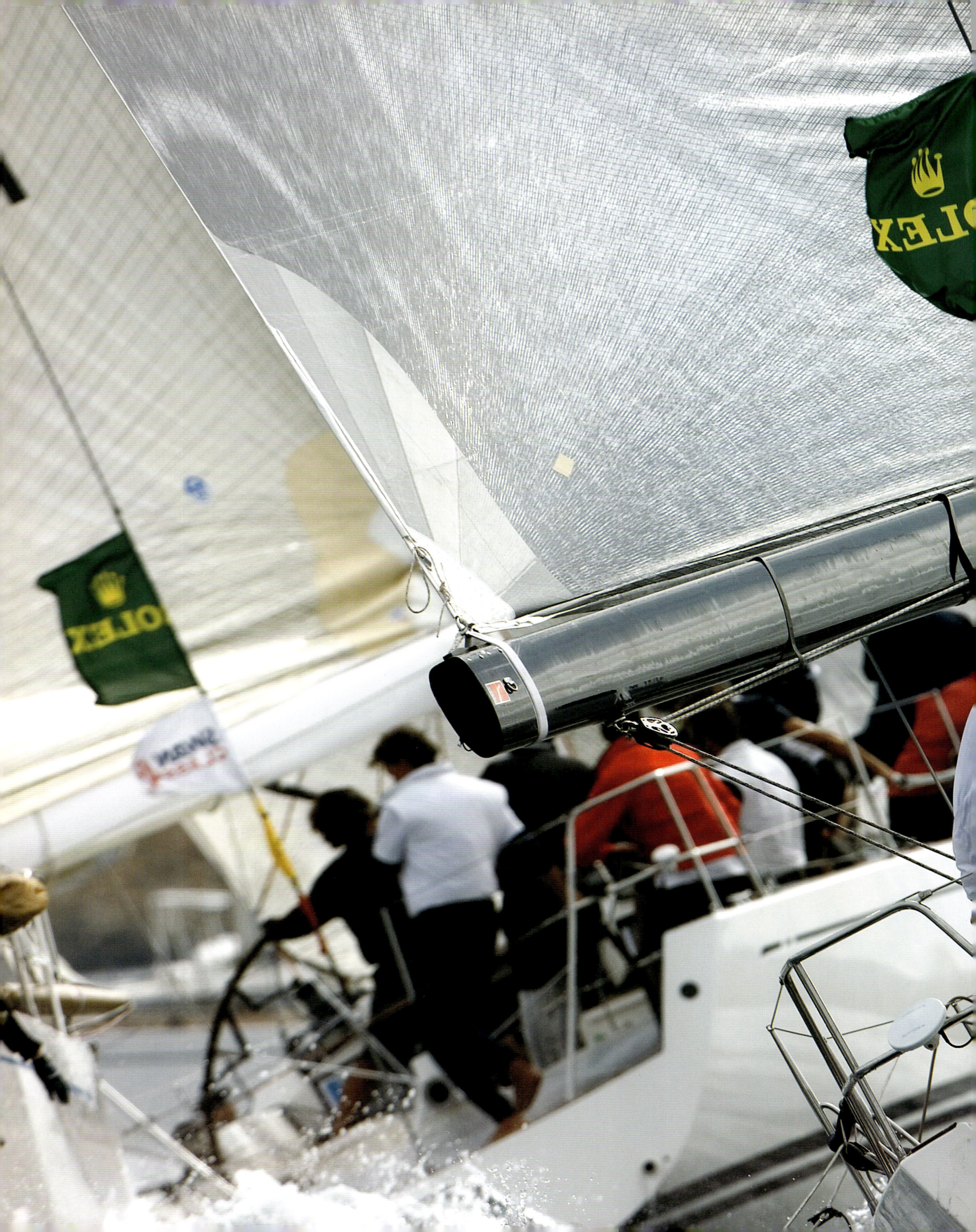

finish of a well-designed and crafted cruising yacht and the pride of ownership that goes with it."[15] The great skipper's practical and deliberately low profile tone only underline his deep involvement.

Third Buoy: Knots
Knots for binding, shortening, stopping, thumb knots... reef knot, fisherman's bend, clove hitch, figure of eight, monkey's fist, bowline: knots are certainly one of the central points of life aboard. Primary technique, original gesture, a writing that preceded signs inscribed on stone,[16] the knot is a puzzle for the inexpert guest and the conjuring trick of the ocean sailor. Tie, undo, tighten, loosen: shipboard life is punctuated by this alternation, this patient and precise activity that does not contemplate the cutting and breaking of life ashore. If things get tangled they are dextrously straightened out. Here there is no place for swords to deal with Gordian knots. The speed of the wind is also measured in knots, and for the superstitious who want to ensure a favourable wind it is indispensable to carry a cord with three knots: undoing the first you get a light breeze; undoing the second you get a good fresh wind; but don't undo the third because it will bring a storm.

The Crew
I give you myself before preaching or law,
Will you give me yourself? Will you come travel with me?
Shall we stick by each other as long as we live?[17]

Owner, skipper, helmsman, bowman, able seaman, cook, cabin boy, guest... different roles, two or three often played by the same person. Crew members carry out different duties but are united by a common fate: aboard they are first and foremost travelling companions. Let's hear their voices: "Human relations are closer at sea due to the shared adventure and the potential danger that always draw people together—sailing is a great way of 'bonding' and crews that have sailed together sometimes remain friends for life," says John Grandy.[18] For Jim Swartz, owner of a Swan 601 and winner of numerous races, they are incomparable relationships "with fun loving sailors. Leave all the worries and baggage behind. Functioning as a team. Wonderful camaraderie."[19] And "light luggage," real and metaphorical, is one of the main features of the "Spirit of Swan." Again: "Aboard a 60 or 80 foot racing yacht in the Southern Ocean crew have to be able to work and live together in harmony in harsh conditions. There is no place for people who are not willing to be part of a team. People have to have absolute faith in their fellow crew members in order to do exactly the right thing in dangerous conditions when they're tired, cold and probably hungry."[20] The boat is an Ark—of safety, of alliance, of pleasure. Harmony and lifestyle aboard are in the hands of the skipper who must become an expert in the difficult art of human relations. "Dealing with men is as refined an art as dealing with ships. Both men and ships live in an unstable element, are subject to arcane and powerful influences and require that their merits be understood rather than their defects exposed."[21]

Fourth Buoy: the Language of the Boat
Shipboard language is precise, as mysterious and fascinating to the neophyte as it is transparent and prescriptive to the expert. An astounding nomenclature which strikes us with its breadth and perfection to the extent of becoming a kind of literary model, of challenging the art of the novelist or poet: "The force, precision

and imagination of a technical language which, created by simple
men whose penetrating eyes grasped the real aspect of the things
of their trade, achieves exact expression in appropriating the
essential: and this is the ambition of the artist of the word."[22]
In the little floating library of a Swan, next to sea and travel
stories, books on marine flora and fauna, pilot books for
the various coasts and a few good thrillers, there will always be
a nautical dictionary, maybe in several languages,[23] so that guests
can practise, experts brush up and kids have fun.

The Voyage: Leaving, Going, Returning

Leaving

I travel not to go anywhere but to go.
I travel for travel's sake.
The great affair is to move.[24]

The mooring lines are cast off and stowed, the quay disappears
from sight, silence on board: the magnetism of departure runs
through the crew. Each one with his questions that flow mute in
the fast, precise gestures of the manoeuvre. "The voyage begins
where our certainties end. Travelling means learning once more
to doubt, to think, to question. Since the frontiers of the
unknown are abolished, travelling means to dare, to challenge
the triteness of the everyday, reassuring comforts, age-old habits.
The voyage is a passage from self to other, the bridge between
two worlds."[25] The moment of departure is the crossing of this
bridge, each separated from the other by a different set of
expectations and anxieties, all brought together by the same
passion. Each has left different things ashore, but on this bridge

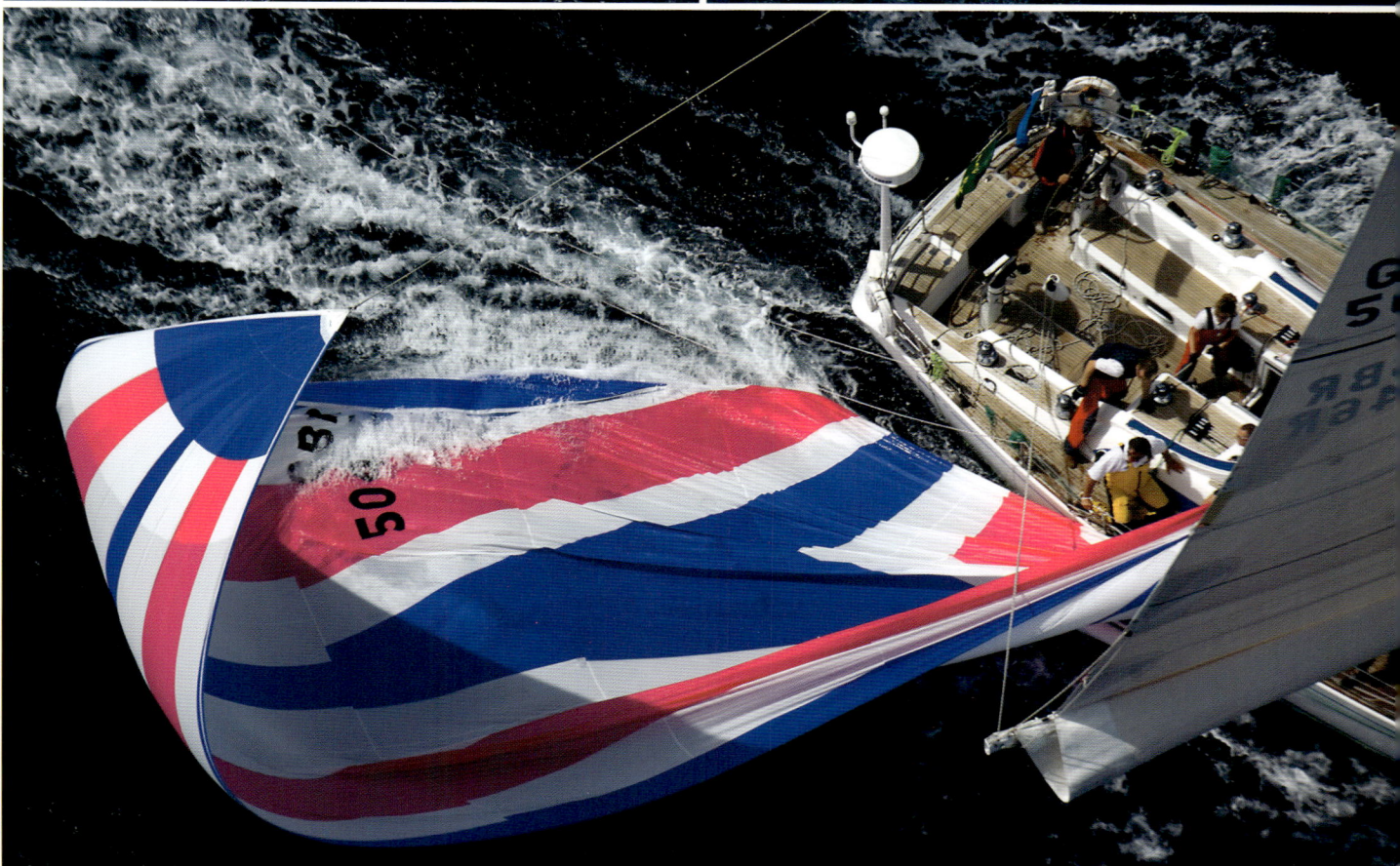

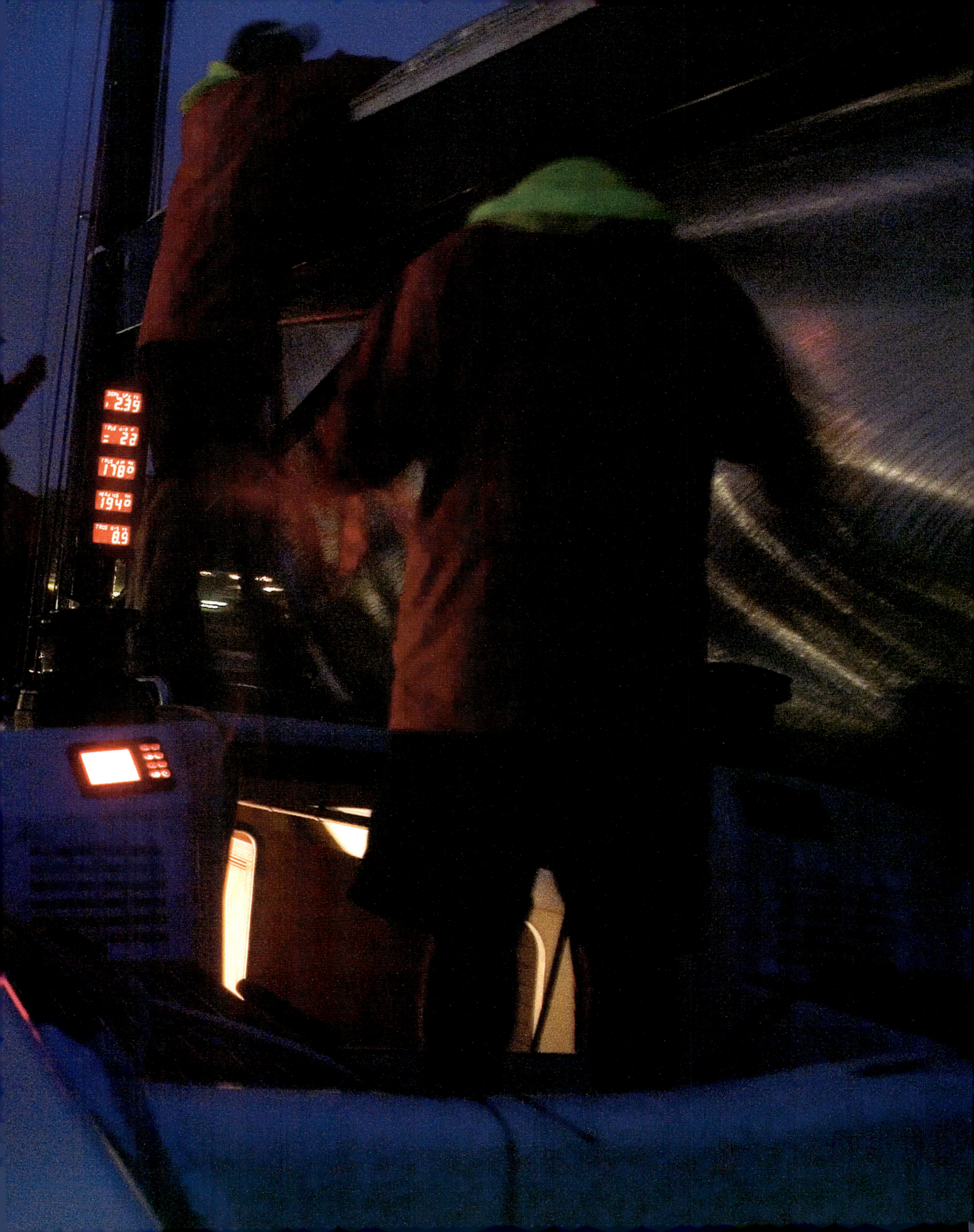
2.39
22
178°
194°
8.9

in the Mediterranean or Sabrina in the Azores.[30] What with floating islands and ghost ships, treasure islands and animated figureheads, the sailor's trust in the objectivity of the chart may well vacillate. Even in the simplest and briefest coastal sailing there's always a moment in which the real place and its position on the chart seem to separate in an irremediable distance.

Going
The fair breeze blew, the white foam flew,
The furrow followed free;
We were the first that ever burst
Into that silent sea.[31]

This is the sensation felt by every sailor on reaching the open sea: though unlike Coleridge's Ancient Mariner we are certainly aware that we are not the first, we nonetheless have the impression that the water, with its ceaseless mobility, is always virgin to us. On the water we leave no lasting traces as on land, our wake is free to disappear in a few moments. Lightened by the liquid element, gravity changes, the point of view changes, becoming mobile and unstable; space is hard to measure by sight without references on land, and time expands. No longer divided and broken up it once more becomes whole like the line of the horizon we are following, becomes eternal where sky meets sea: "It has been found again!/ What? Eternity./ It is the sea fled away/ With the sun," said "the man with soles of wind."[32]
And the space is not that of the yacht—which could appear restricted and constrictive—but the vast space of the sea: the boat is like a second skin, like clothing, only bigger and more

beautiful than clothing, the right clothing for a sea voyage.
"I would say that sailing to me is a must. It is a way of living.
What you learn in your childhood, you do not want to miss
when you grow up. An important thing is that my family loves
sailing too. And I am proud to know that I am the person who
has the longest sailing experience with Swan yachts in the
world,"[33] says Leif Ramm-Schmidt who feels his boat as if it were
an existential shell.

Sixth Buoy: Longitude
For millennia sailors appealed to the sky to show them their
course, but a great many got lost and continued getting lost,
even in the modern age, in spite of Mercator's great
cartographic inventions: though it was relatively easy to
determine latitude, for a long time the problem of longitude
remained unresolved. Sextant and complex calculations of lunar
distance gave results that were too uncertain. Illustrious
astronomers such as Galileo, Newton and Halley tried long
and in vain for a solution in the moon and stars. Then, spurred
on by a considerable reward offered by the English parliament
in 1714, a self-taught watchmaker, John Harrison, came up with
a solution by changing the point of view: each vessel should be
equipped with a chronometer set precisely to London time
(today GMT or UMT, the universal time of the zero meridian).
Comparison with local time, relatively easy to determine, would
immediately indicate the vessel's longitude. The discovery
radically changed sailors' styles and fates.[34] Here are some
amusing quotations on the theme which might sit well near
the chart table of a Swan:
"And navigation make a pleasure
By fynding out the Longitude.

Every Tarpaulin shall then with ease
Sayle any ship to the Antipodes."[35]
"'What's the good of Mercator's North Poles and Equators,
Tropics, Zones and Meridian Lines?'"
So the Bellman would cry: and the crew would reply,
'They are merely conventional signs!'"[36]
"The stars are not wanted now: put out every one;
Pack up the moon and dismantle the sun."[37]
Today we find our position with GPS but—as Joshua Slocum
observed about a hundred years ago—"the calculation of lunar
distances, though rarely practised in our era of chronometers,
is fine and edifying, and nothing exists in the kingdom
of navigation that greater disposes the heart to an act
of adoration."[38] However, let's enjoy the moon and the eyes
of the stars more prosaically without having to decipher them
—but let's keep a good chronometer handy and go back over
the art of the sextant!

Returning
And the end of all our exploring
Will be to arrive where we started
And know the place for the first time.[39]

The yacht returns to port, the line thrown to the quay is the last
of many. Unlike emigration, a voyage of pleasure is by its nature
a round trip: the return is included in the very act of departure.
The adventure is over, you disembark definitively and the land-
sickness seems more intense than what you experienced during
brief times ashore throughout the voyage. The land, so familiar,
seems unknown, unusually hard and rigid, surprisingly new. This

past and distant."[43] Perhaps today, inasmuch as we are tourists, it seems more natural to us to feel nostalgia for the boat and the end of our holiday rather than home and family. Even in the perspective overturned by the paradoxes of modernity, we are still dealing with a return: returning aboard, returning to the open sea to chase the wind. And nonetheless there is a touch of ancient nostalgia in someone who is racing round the world. Grant Dalton states: "There's nothing quite like a finish after 6,000 miles of racing, especially when your family is there."

The race: Participating, Winning, Celebrating

Participating
Play up! Play up! And play the game![44]

"Sailing for me is competition. It is taking your team, your yacht and going out on the race course with other competitors. At the end of the day you have won or lost. The most magical thing about yacht racing, is that each day the field changes. Different breeze. Different sea state. New starting line," says Tom Stark, adding: "During the race, there is only the race. A common goal, a common bond and a common intensity. All else fades as you attend to the task at hand. During the race there is nothing else … The most intense moment is the start of the race. The line is set. The yachts do this elaborate dance trying for the best position. The gun goes off or the horn sounds and it is game on." This is the electrifying atmosphere of ClubSwan, confirmed by all the owners who, lively and enthusiastic, take part in the races held throughout the year. Since the founding of ClubSwan, to safeguard, maintain

and increase the great heritage accumulated over the years,
the races have increasingly become occasions for exchanges
and fun. Crews of all kinds, Swans of different classes and
competitive abilities, all meet to challenge one another in a warm
and cordial atmosphere, like a big family. Days passed at full pace
where you can meet the greats of the international yachting
world and share a lifestyle that blends seafaring tradition
and a fun, relaxed social life.

Eighth Buoy: the Tactician's Tics
A key figure in the race, the tactician observes the water
and the competitors, gathers information from the navigator
and crew, evaluates the situation and takes decisions on race
tactics and strategy. Each tactician has his own specific equipment,
a basic kit that also includes his tics. A typical kit includes: a
wristwatch chronometer with countdown function, a traditional
and/or electronic compass and a bearing compass, a protest flag,
the ISAF Racing Rules (International Sailing Federation), the race
Instructions, a wind direction indicator, a pair of binoculars,
notebook and pencil. Some people add a felt-tip pen, a strategic
checklist and current tables... Some, like Luc Pillot and Philippe
Presti, use alidades previously prepared on film that is stuck
directly onto the deck.[45]

Winning
*The useless and the impossible, these are the truest temptations
of man.*[46]

You go on the water to win, and it doesn't matter how unrealistic
the objective. Right to the end of the race, this is the aim. Taking
the wind out of someone's sails on the race course isn't just

a metaphor! Victory is linked to a good dialectic between technology and the human factor: "Technology is a major part in modern yacht racing. Mastering the technology is as much a part of putting together a winning campaign as selecting the right crew," says Grant Dalton. "A racing yacht is designed and built to achieve an aim—which is to win. I am often in awe of the thought, the skill and work that goes into the design and build of a winning yacht, but all that is for nothing without a skilled and committed crew."[47] With yachts that are increasingly similar in performance and technology, the crew element takes on greater importance, the human factor counting all the more in terms of achieving a result. At the end of the race, an elegant sporting spirit ensures that even defeat can be accepted.

Ninth Buoy: the Protest Flag
Among the many different flags seen waving during a race to signal the most varied situations there is the protest flag. Generally the protest flag is flag "B" of the International Code: red, it signals that you are protesting against another competitor who has broken the rules. Generally the protest flag is made fast to the backstay, rolled up and fixed with Velcro, adhesive tape or cord. Some prefer to fold it accordion style for swift, infallible deployment, while others keep a spare in their pocket just to be on the safe side.

Celebrating
To dance, clap hands, exult,
shout, skip, leap, roll on, float on![48]

It may well be true—as an old proverb says—that "there are no taverns at sea," but with ClubSwan the sea is actually studded

with attractive "taverns": the yachts at the end of a race, ready to welcome friends aboard to celebrate, irrespective of the result, participation in the great game; splendid marinas throughout the world; the numerous festive occasions created by a community of "travellers-players"[49] that is characterised by a strong personality and an unmistakable style. An increasingly full calendar of events, handled by Nautor's Swan system with professionalism and enthusiasm: "When we bought the Swans," says Morten Simon Moe who owns a Swan 53 and a Swan 46, "we also bought a system (agent, yard, ClubSwan). They all give us the feeling of being part of a big family."[50] And in the name of feast, Nautor's Swan's fortieth anniversary has been celebrated: one of the events was the Anniversary Regatta in Finland, a great race amid the twenty thousand islands of the Turku archipelago in the Baltic, in the land and sea where the glorious adventure of Nautor's shipyards began.
The guest of honour and much celebrated *Tarantella*—the Swan of Swans—offered everyone her tireless dance in Swan's first Finnish race.
Other events that celebrate the "Spirit of Swan" are the Rolex Swan Cup, the Swan American Regatta and the Swan European Regatta.

Tenth Buoy: the Story
The voyage, the challenge, the celebration are mythopoeic experiences, generators of narration. It is in their story that they find completion and a new impetus to continue the adventure with other voyages, challenges, celebratory rites. And though when we set about telling the story we often feel inadequate, as if we wanted, in the old Chinese expression, "to measure the ocean with an oyster shell,"[51] it is nonetheless true that precisely

the great stories of sea and coast were the first stimulus, if not the spark, of the desire that sends every sailor to sea. Whether it be oral or written, the story gives meaning to experience, makes it a "shared and spendable value"[52]: between description and invention, between verity and verisimilitude, entrusted to the disguises of memory—"that coin which is never the same," as Borges said—the story is what remains of the experience. No story is possible without a narrator, and the style of the narration is part of the style of the experience. The "Spirit of Swan" is also a great weaver of tales, custodian of adventures of sea and wind, yachts and people, written or yet to be written in the great water of the world.
Maria Sebregondi

¹ In Italian *filo rosso* = red thread. Perhaps a rather worn metaphor but nonetheless pertinent. Here is the origin of the expression: "All the rigging of the royal fleet, from the stoutest to the thinnest, is woven in such a way that a red thread runs through the rope, a thread that cannot be extracted without undoing the whole. So even the smallest fragments can be seen to belong to the crown." Goethe, *Le affinità elettive* [*Elective Affinities*] (1809), Turin 1982, p. 167.

² Jules Michelet, *Il mare* [La mer] (1861), Genoa 1992, p. 277.

³ Jules Michelet, *Op. cit.*, p. 47.

⁴ Jules Michelet, *Op. cit.*, p. 262.

⁵ John Grandy, Interview with the author, April 2006.

⁶ "After years of struggle we realise that we are not the ones who set out on a journey, that it is the journey which sets itself inside us." John Steinbeck, *Travels with Charley*, cit. in Rolf Potts, *Vagabonding*, Italian edition, Milan 2003, p. 61.

⁷ Homer, *Odyssey* X, Italian edition edited by Aurelio Privitera (1981), Milan 1991, p. 281.

⁸ Tom Stark, Interview with the author, April 2006.

⁹ John Grandy, Int. cit.

¹⁰ Edward Fitzgerald, *The Rubaiyat of Omar Khayam*, XXXVII (1859), London 1985.

¹¹ Ernst Aeppli, "I sogni e la loro interpretazione" [Dreams and Their Interpretation] (1943), in Jean Chevalier, Alain Gheerbrant, *Dizionario dei simboli*, Milan 1986, p. 543.

¹² Joseph Conrad, "Epitaffio per l'arte della vela" [Epitaph for the Art of Sail] (1905), in Giampaolo Dossena, Mario Spagnol, *Avventure e viaggi di mare*, Milan 1995, p. 274.

¹³ John Grandy, Int. cit.

¹⁴ Tom Stark, Int. cit.

¹⁵ Grant Dalton, Interview with the author, April 2006.

¹⁶ "Knot writing" is one of the oldest forms of writing, found in pre-Columbian *khipus*: numerous cords of different length, colour and thickness attached along a main cord at varying intervals: various kinds of knots along the cords carry messages in accordance with a code to which the key has been lost.

¹⁷ Walt Whitman, "Song of the Open Road," in *Leaves of Grass* (1855-1891), Turin 1980, p. 195.

¹⁸ John Grandy, Int. cit.

¹⁹ Jim Swartz, Interview with the author, April 2006.

²⁰ Grant Dalton, Int. cit.

²¹ Joseph Conrad, *The Mirror of the Sea*, 1936.

²² Joseph Conrad, in Giampaolo Dossena, Mario Spagnol, *Op. cit.*, p. 287.

²³ A good Italian example, with essential glossary in English and French: Carla Notarbartolo Malingri, Paolo Chighizola, *Dizionario della vela*, Milan 2004.

²⁴ Robert Louis Stevenson, *Travels with a Donkey in the Cévennes*, "Cheylard and Luc," 1879.

²⁵ Franck Michel, *Altrove, il settimo senso. Antropologia del viaggio* (2000), Milan 2001, p. 12.

²⁶ Rosita Forbes, *From Red Sea to Blue Nile* (1925), cit. in Rolf Potts, *Op. cit.*, p. 63.

²⁷ One of the most celebrated cases of serendipity is linked precisely to a great sea voyage: heading west and seeking the Indies, Columbus actually discovered the new world.

²⁸ Paul Theroux, *To the Ends of the Earth* (1990), cit. in Rolf Potts, *Op. cit.*, p. 60.

²⁹ A celebrated statement by Polish semeiologist Alfred Korzybski.

³⁰ Cf. Théodore Monod, "Oceani," in *Enciclopedia*, vol. 9, Turin 1980, p. 965.

³¹ Samuel Taylor Coleridge, *The Rime of the Ancient Mariner*, 1798.

[32] Arthur Rimbaud, *L'éternité*, 1872.

[33] Leif Ramm-Schmidt, Interview with the author, April 2006.

[34] On the history of the discovery of longitude, Cf. Dava Sobel, *Longitudine* [Longitude](1995), Milan 2004.

[35] Anonymous, "Ballad of Gresham College" (ca. 1660), in Dava Sobel, *Op. cit.*, p. 38.

[36] Lewis Carroll, *La caccia allo Snualo* [The Hunting of the Snark] (1876), Pordenone 1990, p. 47.

[37] W. H. Auden, "Canzone" [Song], in Dava Sobel, *Op. cit.*, p. 128.

[38] Joshua Slocum, "Sailing Alone Around the World," in Giampaolo Dossena, Mario Spagnol, *Op. cit.*, p. 263.

[39] T. S. Eliot, *Little Gidding, N° 4 of Four Quartets*, 1942.

[40] Eric J. Leed, *La mente del viaggiatore. Dall'Odissea al turismo globale* [The Mind of the Traveller. History of Travel] (1991), Bologna 1992, p. 354.

[41] *Ibid.*

[42] John Grandy, Int. cit.

[43] Giancarlo Devoto, Gian Carlo Oli, *Il Dizionario della lingua italiana*, Florence 1995.

[44] Henry John Newbolt, *Vitai Lampada* (1897), at www.lib.byu.edu

[45] Didier Ravon and Christian Dumard, *La regata. Tattica e strategia* [La régate. Tactique et stratégie] (2000), Milan 2005, p. 36.

[46] Jules Michelet, *Op. cit.*, p. 201.

[47] Grant Dalton, Int. cit.

[48] Walt Whitman, "A Song of Joys," in *Leaves of Grass*, 1855-1891.

[49] This evocative definition comes from anthropologist Franck Michel who appreciates, in the contemporary traveller, a recovery of the playful and festive spirit. In Franck Michel, *Op. cit.*, p. 79 and subs.

[50] Morten Simon Moe, Interview with the author, April 2006.

[51] This is also the title of an interesting little book edited by Maria Rita Masci (Rome-Naples 1990), a collection of the amazed and perplexed stories of the first Chinese travellers in 19th century Europe.

GOLFO DI TARANTO
Taranto
Paola
Crotone
C. Rizzuto
Stromboli
C. Vaticano
C. Milazzo
Messina
Gioia Tauro
SICILIA
Catania
STRETTO DI MESSINA
C. Spartivento
P. Empedocle
Licata

Today

Success in transforming a logistical difficulty, a company
operating on the outskirts of Europe—and therefore
the world—into the finest yacht manufacturers in the world
is surely the most impressive result of Nautor's Swan shipyard.
When Pekka Koskenkylä began building the Swan 36 in 1966
he certainly had a very broad, advanced and internationalist
vision. He not only chose the New York studio Sparkman
& Stephens, the most acclaimed yacht designers of the day,
but also decided from the start to use fibreglass, a material still
in its infancy for shipbuilding but one which would monopolise
mass production of vessels over the next ten years.
From the origins to 1998 when an epochal event prepared
the yard for entry into the third millennium: it became part
of the group run by Leonardo Ferragamo, an Italian
businessman who has been a Swan owner since the 1980s.
A racing enthusiast, his passion and style represents
the "Spirit of Swan" and membership of an exclusive club
of 1,900 Swan owners.
His main activity in the world of fashion, luxury and "Made
in Italy" exports to the 62nd parallel that magical touch
of "Italian glamour" which, mixed with the long tradition
and technical constructional stability of Pietarsaari, means
that the Finnish yard steps into the 21st century with a breath
of innovation, necessary to keep production in line with
a decidedly altered scenario.
The race towards gigantism that has recently been a feature
of world yachting has led the new owner and the team

of Italian and Finnish managers to extend the building potential of the yard with new premises Nautor in Pietarsaari equipped with modern sheds on an area of 10,000 square metres and the most modern work process machinery.
The premises are on the shore, next to the port of Pietarsaari, and there is a large and efficient marina for launching, testing and mooring large vessels.
The deepest mark left by Italian ownership in this solid Finnish continuity is high technological innovation, with design and construction methods updated to the standards of the 21st century. An automated modelling plant has been installed at the premises in Kållby, 15 kilometres from Pietarsaari. The eight axis FlexMill CNC consists of two robotic arms in parallel on a 30 metre long track on an area 6 metres wide, with a working height of up to 3 metres. The system complements model construction by hand in wood. Working with a polyurethane foam, spread by hand on a base, the finish is precise to a tenth of a millimetre. Time saving is considerable: from a month for the model in wood to a week for the FlexMill version. It takes ten, instead of twenty weeks to complete a male hull. The 3D mathematics used today for designing the whole vessel, from the waterlines to the small details, is sent from the management computer to the robotized arms, which carry out the work process for both hull and small parts. A modular post-cure oven has been set up, expandable to a length of 30 metres and an overall area of 260 square metres. It is used for "post curing" pieces, hulls, decks or small parts,

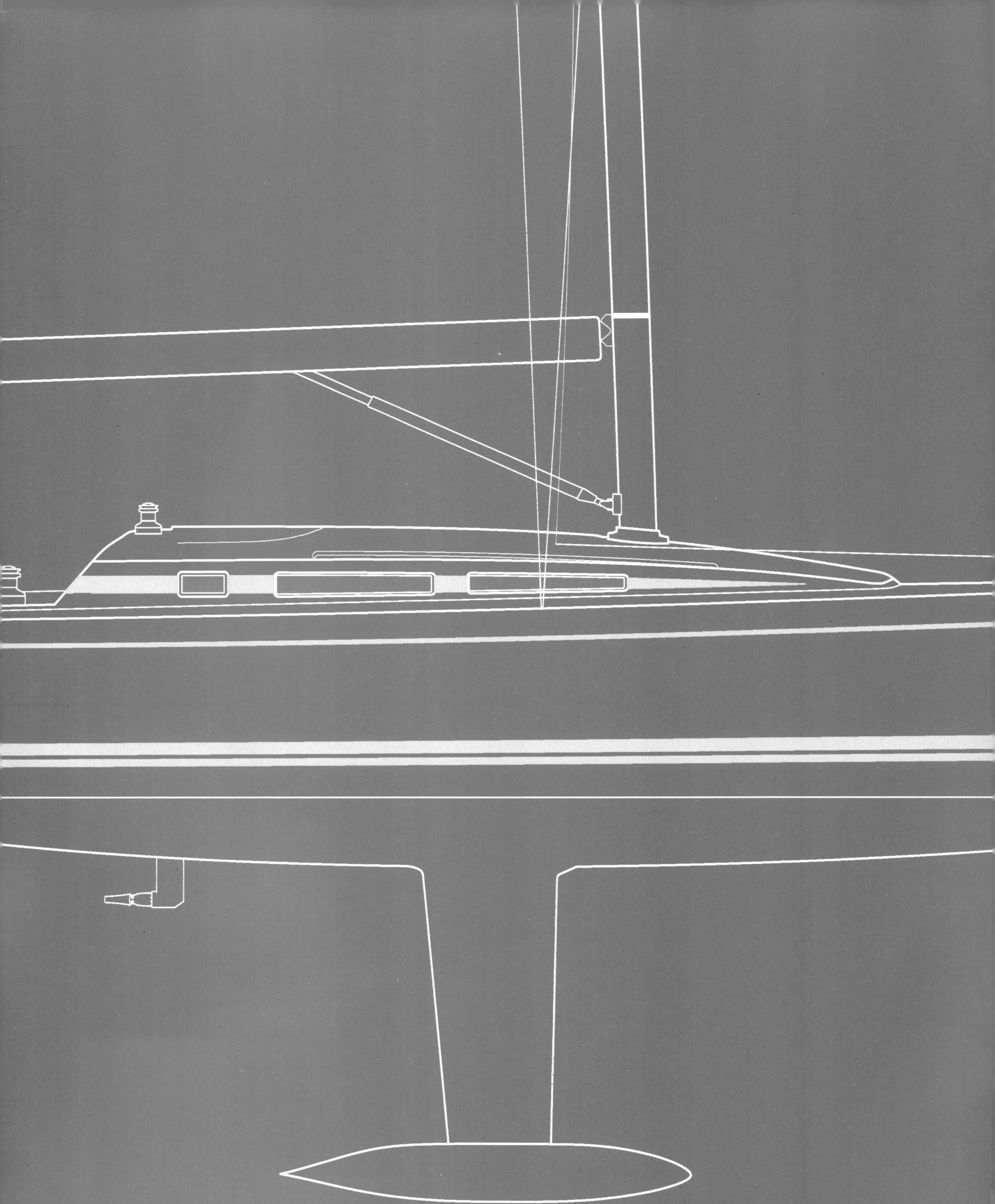

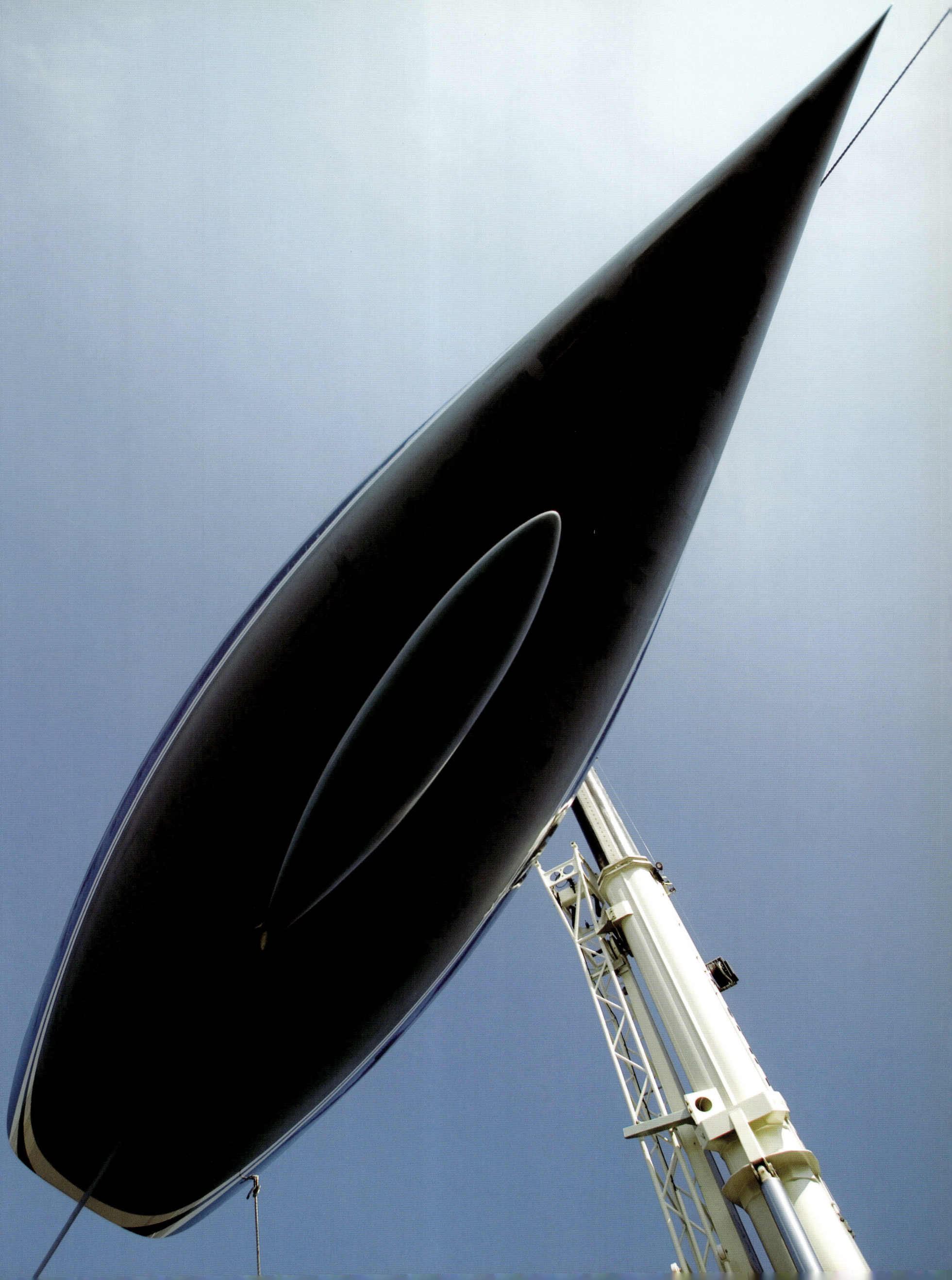

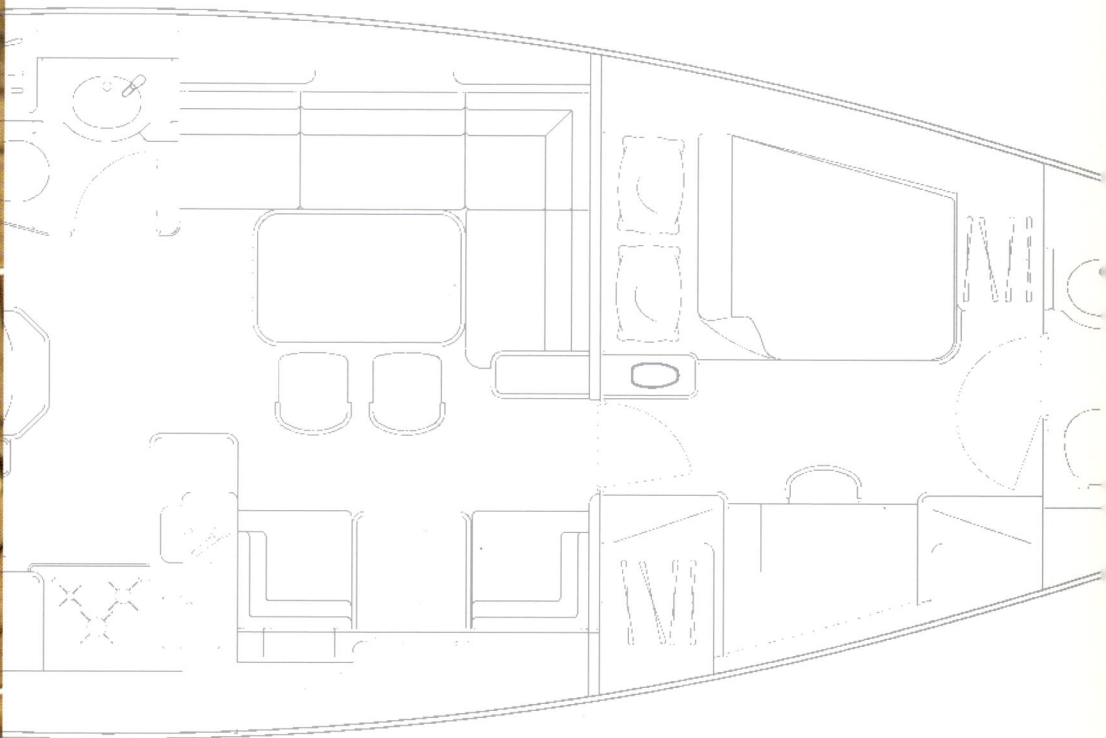

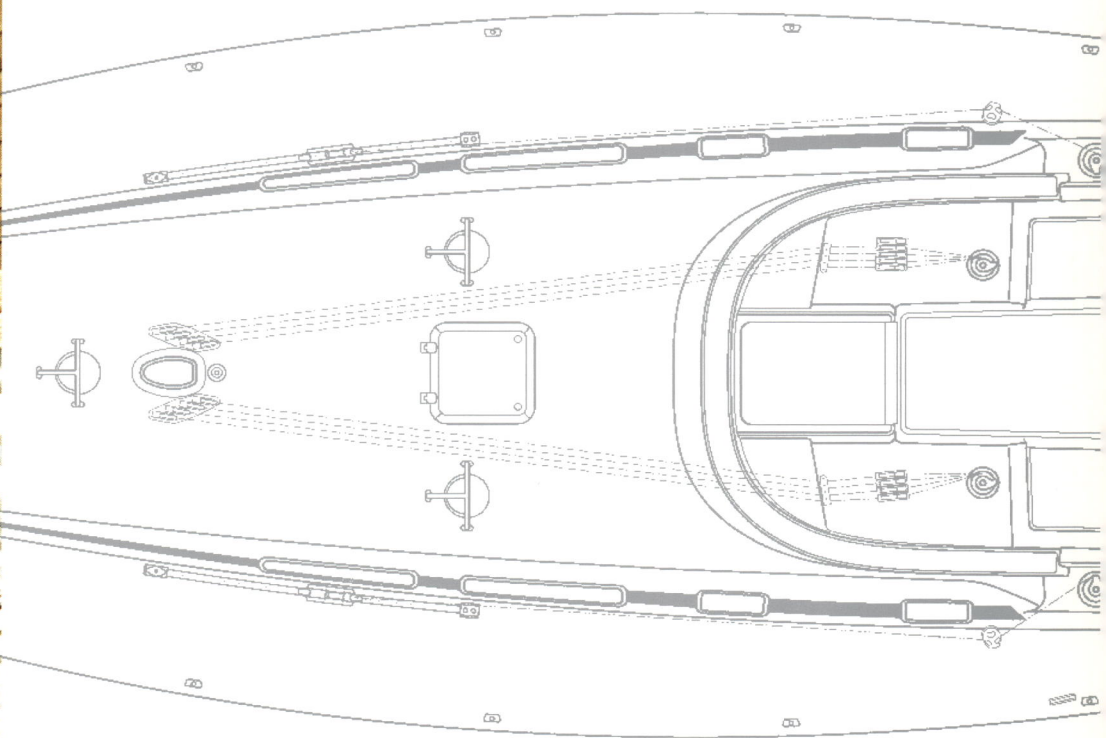

techniques and advanced materials such as reinforcements
in unidirectional carbon fibre, mixed fabrics in fibreglass and
aramid, honeycomb sandwich bulkheads and pre-impregnated
Nomex and with carbon fibre. The result is a light, tough hull,
even more robust than the proverbial Nautor solidity.

The most innovative model in this range is the brand new
Swan 90, the first hull completely modelled by the robotized
arms of the FlexMill and built completely with the infusion
technique: 27.73 metres LOA, beam 6.46 metres, length-beam
ratio 4.44, displacement 52 tons, ballast at 38 per cent with
T shaped keel. A real thoroughbred with flush deck, the best
of German Frers' expressive capabilities and the best
constructional skills upgraded to Nautor's most advanced
technology.

The second area deals with custom yachts, great sailyachts
which, with new technologies and the big new Nautor premises
by the sea, are produced in a range of 100 to 131 footers.
These Swans—they're still called Swans—have hulls, waterlines
and sail plans researched, defined and designed by German
Frers together with the yard's technicians.

They offer owners plenty of deck plan options, from flush deck
to raised saloon, various interior layouts and high
customisation in terms of systems, décor, wood and finishes.
The Swan 100 is an interesting member of this range:
30.21 metres LOA, beam 7.06 metres, length-beam ratio 4.27
and 70 tons displacement, available in flush deck, semi-raised
saloon and raised saloon versions and different interior layouts.

It has had great success as no less than seven yachts had been ordered by the end of 2005.

The first megasailer of this series was the Swan 112: 34.34 metres LOA, beam 7.42 metres, 129 tons displacement, sloop rig with a 40.80 metre mast and a sail area of 485 square metres on a run. A real superyacht with an immense owner's suite, only two spacious guest cabins and a vast raised saloon with a fine sea view, thanks to extensive glazed areas.

The "Spirit of Swan" is still total, and the image, substance and general concept still perfectly legible and identifiable, dimensions notwithstanding. Even in the gigantism of the first Swan 131 (40 metre), the biggest ever built, with interiors designed by Dick Young: 200 tons displacement, 741 square metres of sail area, sloop rigged with a 50.32 metre mast and two 490 HP engines.

The third area deals with monotype classes. Pure racing machines in the power of their waterlines and sail plan, but still Swans as far as interior quality, comfort and elegance are concerned. The first model in this innovative category, which was nevertheless closely linked to the sporting origins of the Swan family, was the Swan 45 which in 2006, after only four years, already has more than fifty examples launched: 13.83 metres LOA, beam 3.91 metres with a length-beam ratio of 3.53, racing displacement 8,850 kilos with 44.2 per cent ballast, the Swan 45 has been highly appreciated by Mediterranean, Northern European and American owners happy to sail a real, powerful racer, as exciting as a dinghy, in the fleet and without handicap.

Having set the trend, Nautor—with the enthusiasm of Enrico Chieffi and the impetus provided by German Frers who strongly believed in the one-design choice—launched the Swan 601 in 2004 which won the American IRC championship, beating customised one-off racers. 18.30 metres LOA, beam 4.54 metres, length-beam ratio 4.03, displacement 18 tons with 48.33 per cent ballast, the Swan 601 concentrates all the new technologies. Extensive use of carbon and infusion resulted in a tough and very light hull—as seen from the ballast weight—but as with every Swan nothing was skimped on the high class interiors. There are three different layouts. The third example of the monotype series is the Club Swan 42, designed by Frers Design Office and the yard for the New York Yacht Club.

The Yacht Club of 44th Street has always had a monotype "Club Boat" for races between members. In autumn 2004 the NYYC decided to begin the study of a new "Corinthian" class, which is to say strictly for amateur racing with a dilettante crew and a "gentleman helmsman," the latter generally the club member. Nautor and the Frers studio put together a solid team who devised a "fine sailer" that fulfilled the always very high expectations of NYYC members, in the Swan tradition and with the new technologies and construction capacities available to the yard today: 12.98 metres LOA, beam 3.93 metres, length-beam ratio 3.30, displacement 6,885 kilos with 46.4 per cent ballast, the Club

Swan 42 has a T shaped keel, draught of 2.70 metres and a great reduction of weight due, precisely, to high-tech building techniques. Frers' VPP envisaged very high performances even close-hauled in light winds. Dozens of Club Swan 42 were sold immediately and the yacht would be adopted by other clubs for class racing.

A consolidated structuring of production, development of advanced plant and technologies, forty years of experience and almost 2,000 vessels built (from 11 to 40 metres) led to the idea of sharing this vast, in-depth across the board know-how outside the production lines linked strictly to the "Spirit of Swan."

So the Custom division came into being, putting the yard's skills on the market for the building of "fine sailers" of every kind. A top-line shipyard where the future owner can go with his architect and designer to have his own fully made to measure yacht built. This opening up to the global market was a further evolution of the yard's desire to employ its experience in building vessels of high technical value.

The first signs of the Custom division date back to 1986 when Ron Holland, whom the yard had engaged for mass production of his Imp 40 that won the 1977 Fastnet, designing a total of six models between 37 and 44 feet, designed the Garuda 102: 31 metres, 113 tons, the biggest sailyacht in composite of its time, with hull and deck in Airex sandwich and skins in vacuum bagged carbon and aramid.

Twenty years later Nautor is involved in building a 76 footer

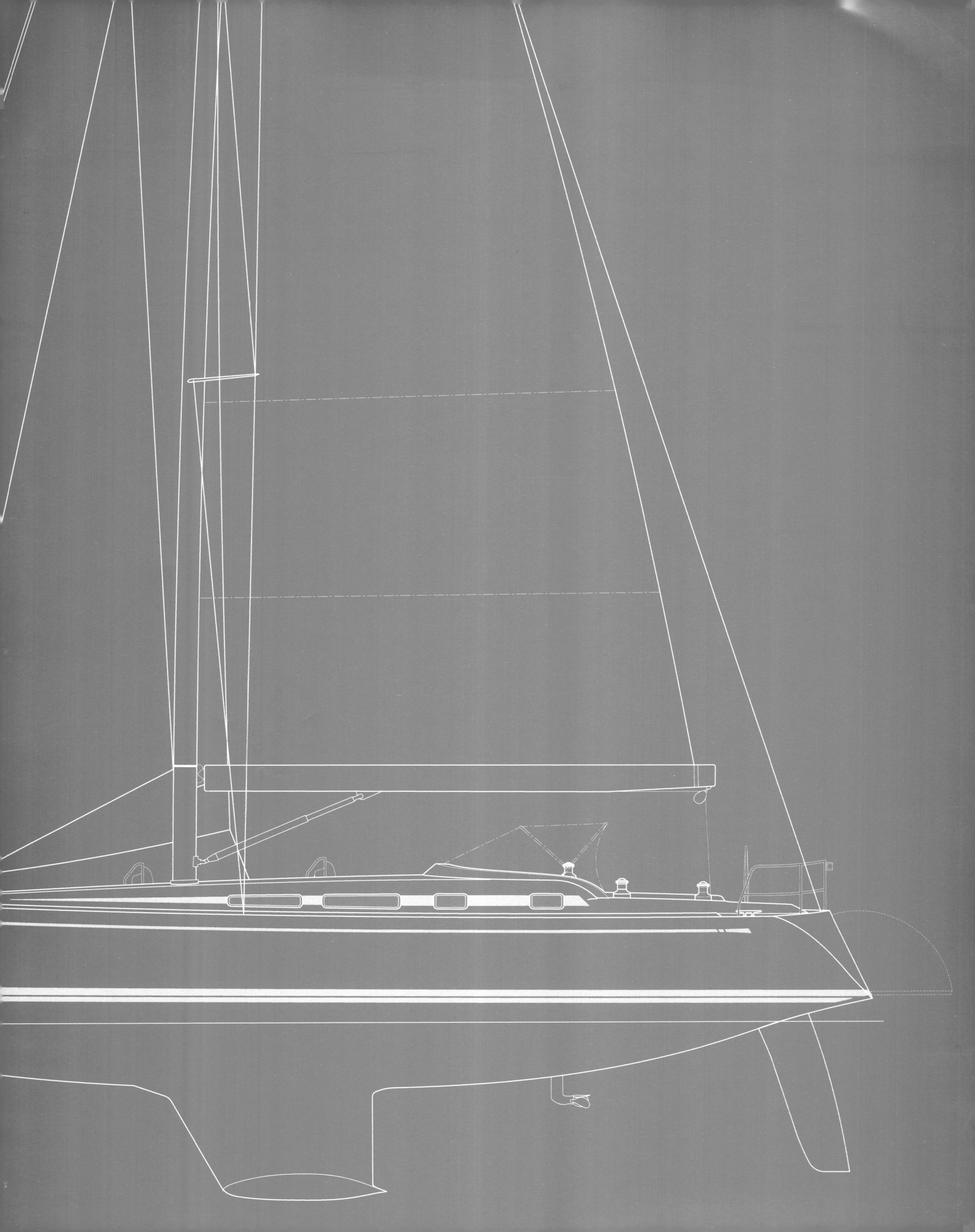

"He always thought of the sea as *la mar* which is what people call her
in Spanish when they love her. Sometimes those who love her say bad things
of her but they are always said as though she were a woman.
Some of the younger fishermen … spoke of her as *el mar*, which is masculine.
They spoke of her as a contestant or a place or even an enemy.
But the old man always thought of her as feminine
and as something that gave or withheld great favors, and if she did wild
or wicked things it was because she could not help them.
The moon affects her as it does a woman, he thought."

(Ernest Hemingway, *The Old Man and the Sea*, 1952)

the yard world famous over the last forty years.

The coloured gelcoat—be it for the hull, the side stripes or the waterline—is applied by brush to achieve higher quality and greater thickness of the coat. It lasts longer and it's brighter.

The furniture is built in the carpentry workshops in Kronoby. The material is teak. The veneers are made in-house using an increasingly varied number of woods. The veneer laminations are hot-bent with a press into specific forms.

The material is purchased on selected markets by a buyer, and when a substantial batch is available it is bought quickly and stored for seasoning in an air-conditioned warehouse.

Varnish is spray-applied in several coats—dining tables get more coats—with sanding between coats with progressively finer sandpaper, thus assuring the velvety, semi-gloss finish that has always characterised the Swans of Finland.

The finishing of teak decks are handled through outsourcing within the shipyard. With headquarters next to the Nautor Pietarsaari, another company produces masts in aluminium and carbon fibre, satisfying Nautor's requirements for series production and custom yachts, masts which just a few years ago were wholly constructed within the yard. The company's track record includes high-tech top performance spars for traditional and classic vessels.

But over and above its strong innovative currents, robotizing, outsourcing and customisation, Nautor remains a great "town within a town" and gives employment to 450 families.

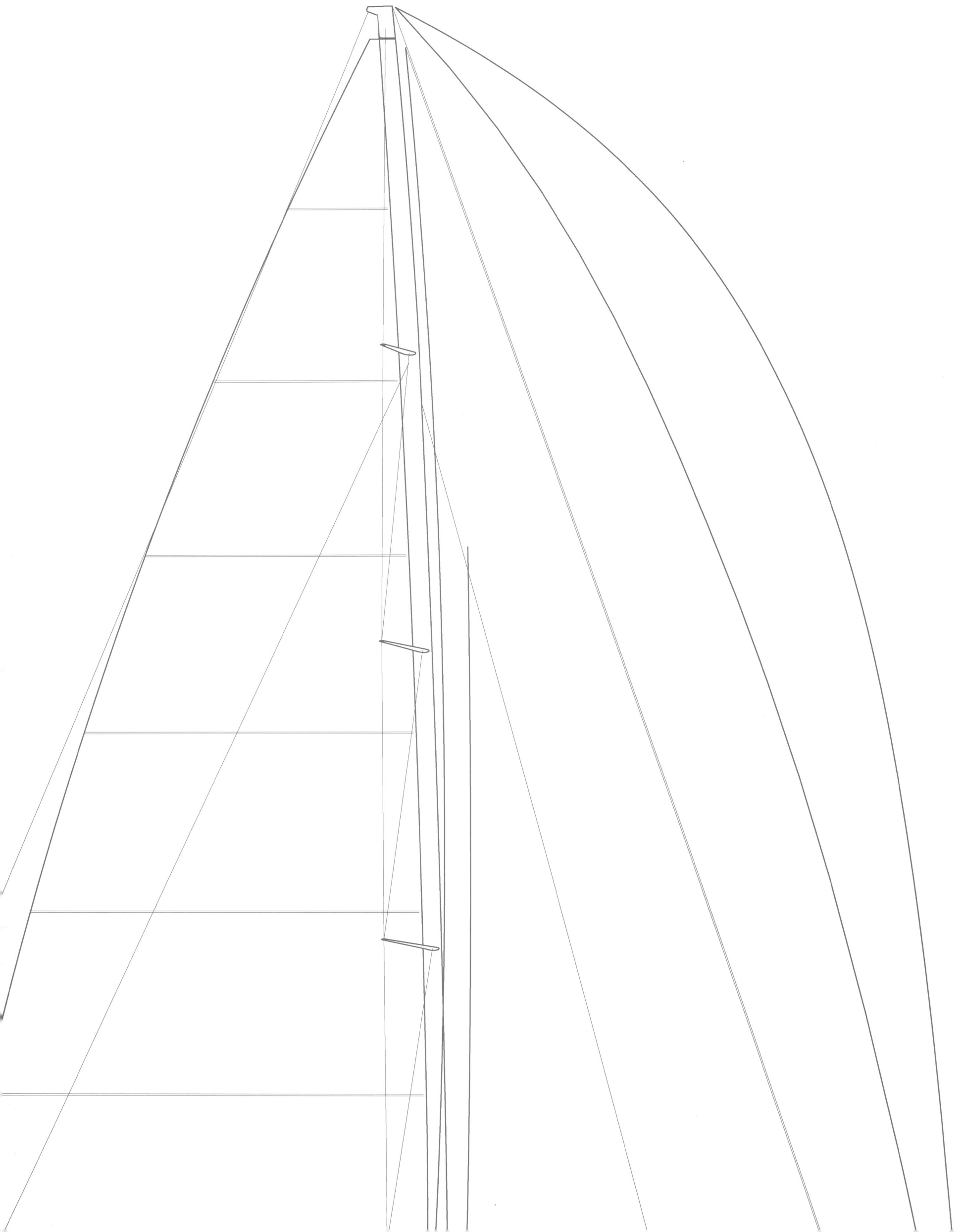

Pietarsaari

Previous pages New Nautor facility in Pietarsaari. / New Nautor facility and Marina in Pietarsaari. Swan 131. Moulding department.

Assembly of the bulkheads. / *Following pages* Swan 131.

The parallel is certainly not a chance one when the poetics of both occurrences, the one narrated and the other about everyday life, is one and the same: the bitter climate of Finland. In Arto Paasilinna's story the hot water, poured in bucketfuls over the rolls of bituminised felt, frees them from the ice that prevents their being laid on the hut roof. Similarly the hot water which the UPM Kymmene paper-mill and the Electric Power Station discharge copiously into the sea keeps a stretch of water free from the ice that closes the port of Pietarsaari during the long winter. Magical impact: just as the bituminised felt becomes soft and workable, so does the sea, constrained to immobility, open up before the new premises of Nautor in

NORRFIBER

Oven.

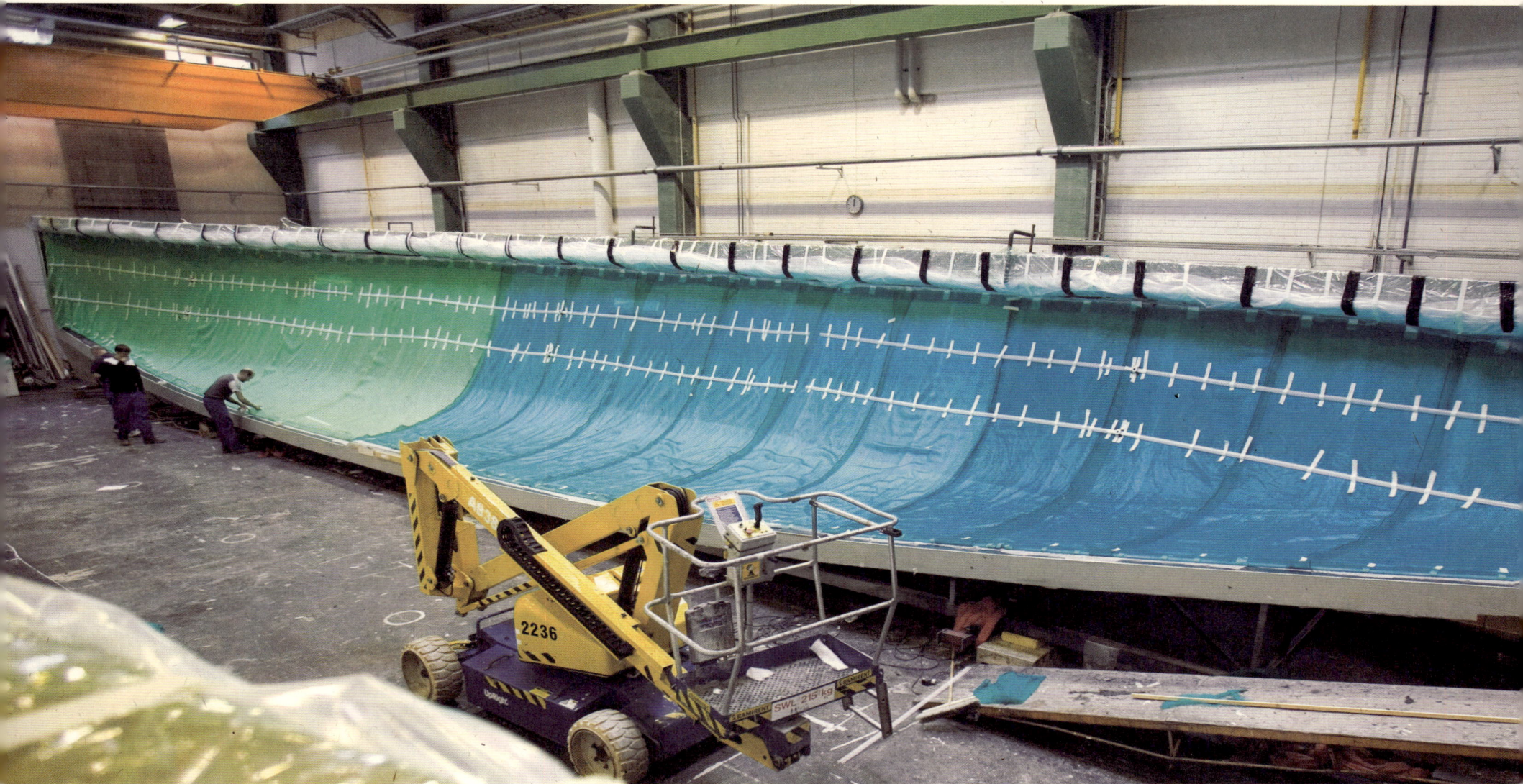

Swan 90: infusion in Kållby.

Pietarsaari with a private marina. This means that vessels, especially large ones, can be put into the water for trials and mooring and prepared for taking to sea when the season changes.

In the new centre a team of technicians are testing the latest technologies, perfecting the special Nautor design identity. Design criteria excludes solutions that might be short lived, and only appropriate innovations are employed. This is how the Italian owner acts like a midwife today, in relation to the construction ethic, to the innate stubbornness of the Finns, opening up new fronts to the expert technicians and entire workforce.

Moulding department: FlexMill working at the deck mould. Launch of Swan 100 S, Aquarius Alfa.

The original Nautor premises in Kållby.

The new Nautor facility in Pietarsaari is the head office and handles all assembly. Lamination and moulding take place in the traditional Kållby premises.

A fascinating rigour of processes that result in defining the form of each individual unit: there is a strong sense of tradition, dating back to very remote times. The Kållby premises also has a section dedicated to producing teak decks. Originally, the planks were fixed by screws but today they are glued and stand out well in the design of the surfaces.

Workers in Kållby: spar and assembly departments.

In the premises at Kronoby (carpentry department) the art lies in concretising components and furnishings which, assembled aboard, constitute the outstanding living spaces, recognised for their comfort.

The technicians and workforce demonstrate great know-how, which is manifested in their methods of execution and the resulting work has a superior quality. Wood is the prince of materials, and a variety including cherry, maple, oak and teak are used on flat surfaces and alluring curves. Meticulousness and unparalleled attention to detail are unmistakable facts.

Spar and metal shop departments.

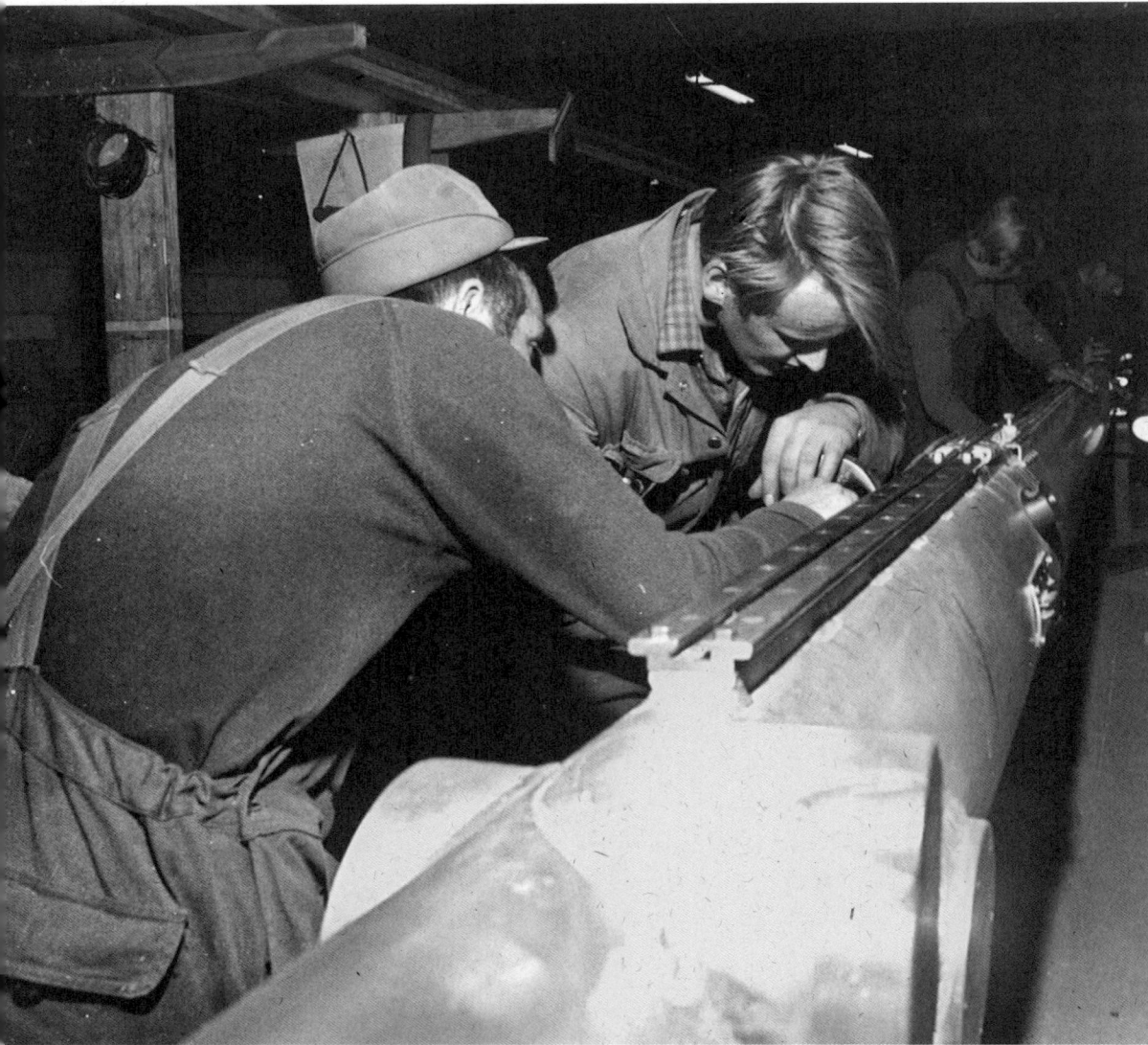

Wood samples from all of the vessels are preserved. This method prevents the unpleasant impact of contrasting colours, veining and veneer irides-cence in the case of replacement or touch-up of the parts most subject to wear.
The three premises of the Nautor yard work closely together, on the design and creation of products that are distinguished by their excellence worldwide.
Decio Giulio Riccardo Carugati

Yesterday

"The dullest of folk cannot see this kind of thing hour after hour
through long days without noticing it; and … comprehend
and enjoy the dry chorus of wave-tops turning over with a sound of incessant
tearing; the hurry of the winds working across open spaces and herding
the purple-blue cloud-shadows; the splendid upheaval of the red sunrise."

(Rudyard Kipling, *Captains Courageous*, 1897)

permeates the seafaring tradition of the Baltic coast where going
to sea is no simple matter and vessel reliability is a proverbial
condition. In this context the excellence of Nautor was established
in 1966 and subsequently developed with the founding of the
yard of the same name and production of the splendid, inimitable
Swans. The summa of continuity, coherence and consistency, but
equally of lightness, elegance and beauty, the Swans took their
place on the world's oceans at the peak of Nautor know-how.
The design of the vessels is a fruitful collaboration between
Nautor's Swan and the best designers of all time. The relationship
is still, above all, a design in design.
"Myth is a word," notes Roland Barthes in *Mythologies*, "but
of course not just any word: language requires special conditions
in order to become myth—myth is a system of communication,
a message. Every object in the world may pass from a closed, mute
existence to an oral state, open to society's approval, because
there is no law, natural or otherwise, to prevent us speaking
about things."
It's easy to explain what inspired Pekka Koskenkylä to set up
Nautor in Edsevö. Firstly, his knowledge of the territory, then
his indispensable sailing experience and, lastly, his desire to build
that first yacht suitable for racing and blue water sailing, fully
equipped for this twofold purpose. Koskenkylä predicted that
more than one owner in the international field might identify
with this desire to own such a boat. A chance not to be missed,
it gave Koskenkylä the opportunity to communicate and
demonstrate the excellence of Finnish shipbuilding everywhere
he went.
For that first model, the Swan 36 destined for series production,
Koskenkylä entrusted the design to the Sparkman & Stephens
studio in New York, where Olin and Rod Stephens had already

features curved lines and flat forms. The organic drawing
of his lines is rooted in nature and is expressed with the power
of elementary forms."
He investigates tastes and experiments with the organic material
par excellence—wood—and studies its constructional possibilities.
To this end he exploits the humidity of the wood fibre, especially
birch which is widespread in Finland. He moves from free formal
research to the devising of useful forms, by which he means
furniture, objects and fittings, all accessories to the overall
architectonic plan aimed at the most welcoming result.
"As has been noted," comments Renato De Fusco in *Storia
del Design* (History of design), "Aalto's interest in the item
of furniture concerns a formal problem and its relationship with
man's behaviour and reactions, which has precedence over special
solutions of execution required by the design or the subsequent
choices of product distribution. So the Aalto object, designed
for specific environments, has no interest in mass production
in the current sense of the term and envisages a possibility of
standardisation linked solely to the design components, conceived
in terms of an architecture and a dialectic relationship between
man and environment." Thus Aalto's furniture in birch, his objects,
his glass vases still stand out today for "the power of elementary
forms."
Materials and the study thereof mediate, lend behaviour, ensure
the complete reliability of all artifices. Aalto does not oppose his
action of devising but sets up a dialogue charged with poetics,
easily recognised in the culture of his land where research
and method are essential data in the relationship between man
and environment, when man's action in the latter has always
been inspired by the criteria of survival.
A culture of understanding, not breach of trust, moreover

Both have three double cabins, offering owner and guests
a deck layout of great comfort with plenty of space
in the cockpit and on the deckhouse: a profiled and practical
sprayhood, perfectly integrated into the arched line
surrounding the entrance, a refined and cultured reference
by German Frers to classic solutions dating to the 1960s.
The new Swan 66 is being created to mark the 40th
Anniversary of Nautor's Swan. This elegant design has all
the qualities associated with Nautor's Swan and it shares many
similarities with the legendary Swan 65 of the 1960s.
The parameters of these two models are altogether different:
20.15 metres LOA, beam 5.39 metres, length-beam ratio 3.74,
displacement 30 tons with ballast at 31 per cent and a draught
of 3.20 metres (standard version) and 3.80 metres for the racing
version. There is also a shallow draught drop-keel version
for pure cruising.
There are two interior layouts: owner's cabin aft and two
cockpit deck; or owner's cabin forward and single cockpit deck.
Extensive use of carbon fibre, monolithic or sandwich, means
an extraordinary tough and light structure.
The first large size model, and the first of a successful series,
was the Swan 82: 24.89 metres LOA, beam 5.86 metres,
length-beam ratio 4.24, displacement 38 tons, available in three
deck versions—flush deck, raised saloon and semi-raised
saloon—and in different interior layouts. A yacht suitable
for fast cruising, she always holds her own in the Swan races.
The Swan 82 was the first to be built using new construction

requiring a phase of heating to perfect polymerisation.
The same plant is also used to "post cure" pieces—hulls,
decks or small parts—laminated with the infusion process
and requiring a special treatment to achieve proper curing
of the resin.
There are many advantages to lamination and have to do with
the quality of the piece and of the work environment. Styrene
emissions are practically nil and several hulls may be produced
with the same mould.
The important innovations in plant and the developing of the
most advanced technologies permit the shipyard to tackle new
and significant challenges in order to arrive at even greater
achievements as its history develops.
Over the years production has been split into three
fundamental areas. The most classic deals with performance
cruisers, the roots of Nautor and the imprinting of the Swans.
They are the same pure Swans, updated by German Frers'
creativity and by new technologies. The range comprises the
Swan 46, the Swan 53, the Swan 66, the Swan 70, the Swan 75,
the Swan 82 and the Swan 90.
The "cubs" of the range are the Swan 46 and the Swan 53,
a contemporary reinterpretation of the most classic Swans
of the 1980s and 1990s, again of course the work of Frers who
has designed a delicately evolved line which however can
accommodate all of the latest expedients for fast, comfortable
cruisers, including the double helm station and the transom
that opens up to form a handy bathing platform.

therefore the yacht that best responded to the expectations of the moment. There were different solutions for the owner's cabin: central double bed with semicircular sofas, or two separate beds in accordance with the classic Swan style, a double on the starboard side and a single on the port.

Access to the bathroom/shower is direct in both cases. The galley is in the passageway between the aft cabin and the saloon, the latter in a regular design with a sofa opposite the C shaped dinette. Upper berths may alternatively be transformed into open lockers. Forward the quarters include a second head and the cabin may have two foldaway bunks in tubular metal and canvas, serving also as a sail-store or be fitted with a double bed and semicircular sofa.

As for the rigging, the mast has shrouds in discontinuous rod with head foil, running backstay and inner forestay. A hydraulic tensioner regulates the backstay and the central unit is equipped for a hydraulic vang. On request a small coffee grinder with pedestal could be added forward of the mainsail traveller. Draught is 1.75 metres (Scheel keel) and 1.70 to 2.90 metres (drop-keel). Nautor also supplied a racing version with a three spreader mast, running backstay, hydraulic unit for backstay, head foil, inner forestay and vang.

With the Swan 60 German Frers anticipated the formal and substantial features of the latest generation performance cruisers. "Yachts," he comments, "designed for long ocean-going sailing, right down to the smallest detail, from maximum living comfort to ease of manoeuvre, thanks to the adoption of ad hoc technologies. But also ready for racing. I've always designed boats to be sailed, never to be left on show tied up at the dockside. When an object is conceived for sailing, its beauty is the expression of an intimate excellence, not the vulgar stereotype

of appearances. Right from the first model, the Swan 46, I've tried
and I am still trying today to deliver a synthesis of the Nautor
cultural tradition and the most up to date design, for the best
signification of the family line, of its continuity. I observe one
of my new yachts, I recognise her, she's a Swan and I'm proud
to have designed her."

Each Swan represents the uniqueness of a way, a behaviour, where
the design is within the design. Each Swan is a yacht devised by
and for someone who loves the sea. "Our yachts," Enrico Chieffi
points out, "cross oceans. Their owners are our true promoters.
They communicate and perpetrate the Nautor myth worldwide.
Right from the founding of the yard, from that first spark in the
white Baltic Sea, the Swan 36. The owners, then, are the real
chiefs of Nautor. Today production includes three sections of
design development: performance cruiser, one-design and custom.
The first is in the name of continuity of guidelines that have never
been disregarded. An unmistakable identity, the essence of Swan
configuration, where yachts are created to be sailed fast, with
high performance but with equally high levels of comfort
in the living quarters. Sailing with a Swan excludes all
compromises in a choice of quality. The second perfects the
uniqueness of the design of a yacht built for competition racing,
and here each example is rigorously identical. The third gives
the world's owners the chance to create big yachts to their own
specifications, exploiting Nautor's design and productive skills.
Each commission is an enviable acknowledgement, from customers
who could easily look elsewhere, of the consummate expertise of
the technicians and workforce of a yard that can boast a princely
product, the Swan series, yachts admired worldwide by those who
love the sea."

Love for the sea is a timeless love. "The sea! the sea! the open

sea!," Bryan W. Procter wrote. "The blue, the fresh, the ever free!/ Without a mark, without a bound,/ It runneth the earth's wide regions round!/ It plays with the clouds; it mocks the skies;/ Or like a cradled creature lies./ I'm on the sea! I'm on the sea!/ I am where I would ever be;/ With the blue above, and the blue below,/ And silence wheresoe'er I go."

"The Finns' main gifts," continues Enrico Chieffi, "are constancy, method, order and a maniacal attention to detail. On the other hand, the extreme climatic conditions forbid approximation and everything produced by man must be safe, efficient and reliable. The necessity to exclude error is translated into excellence of method, into the most rigorous constructional ethic. We see that the Swan myth is fully justified. Thanks to information technology and the most advanced electronics we are able to reconstruct the case history of every single unit and, from launching onwards, monitor its behaviour. So we can supply the owner with an exhaustive picture of the vessel in question, suggesting maintenance phases and time schedules as well as places where these operations can be carried out. This system stands strictly on the reliability of the building criteria and processes of Nautor yachts."

Joseph Conrad wrote: "As if it were too great, too mighty for common virtues, the ocean has no compassion, no faith, no law, no memory. Its fickleness is to be held true to men's purposes only by an undaunted resolution and by a sleepless, armed, jealous vigilance … Unlike the earth, it cannot be subjugated at any cost of patience and toil."

"In the north the sea is certainly not as agreeable as ours or other seas," says Leonardo Ferragamo. "It's demanding as well as cold, it freezes over for long periods of the year. Pride in what they do well, such as boatbuilding, is a characteristic feature of the Finns.

For many years a Swan was my unachievable dream. And here
I have to say that when I decided to purchase Nautor in 1998,
I would never have made such a commitment to any other yard.
Immediately afterwards, all the Swan enthusiasts realised that
behind my decision there was an entrepreneurial plan, a vision,
above all determination in the long term.
My intention from the start was to integrate the two cultures,
Italian management and Finnish design and production. With
products so reliable, so well made, so safe, we made our
contribution in areas where Italians are among the best,
marketing above all, for a dynamic, modern vision of the
approach. Certainly I also transfused my personal experience, my
sensitivity to the beautiful but equally to the well crafted object.
Today, in the opinion of third parties, Nautor is world leader
throughout the nautical sector in terms of brand appeal.
Maintaining leadership means managing your strong points,
making them evolve. This is our challenge." When "myth is a
word, not just any word," Nautor's Swan is a message of passion,
and ever more topical.
Decio Giulio Riccardo Carugati

Bibliography
Roland Barthes, *Mythologies, Paris 1957*.
Werner Blaser, *Il design di Alvar Aalto*, Milan 1981.
Joseph Conrad, *The Mirror of the Sea*, London 1906.
Renato De Fusco, *Storia del design*, Rome-Bari 1998.
Elias Lönnrot, *Kalevala*, London-Helsinki 1835.
Arto Paasilinna, *The year of the Hare*, London 2006.
Bryan W. Procter, *English Songs*, Boston 1851.

"I was a boy of sixteen," says Matteo Salamon, "with a great passion for all yachts, for Swans, one in particular, the 1972 Sparkman & Stephens Swan 38. I said to myself then: when I grow up... And at last in 1999 I was able to realise my dream, buying a Swan 38 series 1976, in optimal condition, from her third owner. I can still say today that to live a love, so long dreamt of, is the greatest emotion when, as in the case of Swan, the extreme elegance of the form corresponds to absolute structural perfection, the beauty corresponds to safety and reliability. I decided to organise exchanges with owners worldwide who share my passion for vintage Swans by setting up the S&S Swan Association, open to owners of the Sparkman & Stephens series. I've created a website where associates can exchange experiences, ranging from the pleasure of sailing to the restoration and maintenance of these authentic gems.

A fundamental rule governs our meetings: the owner or one of his family must be at the helm. We had our most recent meeting in 2005, a few miles north of Punta Ala, with the patronage of Nautor's Swan and thirty-two vessels in the roadstead. An unforgettable spectacle, ah, that fleet of Swans, in the evening, motionless on the water." See how a word, Swan, is certainly not just any word, it is inimitable way and form.

In the second half of the 1970s, with the advent of a new generation of designers who monopolised the top of the racing classifications, the scenario progressively changed. With an eye for innovative solutions Ron Holland showed that he well knew how to interpret the most advanced technological propositions. In 1977 he designed the high performance Imp, resolved in attention to structural technical details and the correct relationship between exterior and interior design. In the same year the yacht took part in the SORC and the Admiral's Cup.

Nautor's Swan management approved the collaboration with this designer who best distinguished himself at the time in development of the racer configuration. In 1978 Holland created the Swan 39 series version, racing and cruising, of that fortunate model for the Finnish yard. The deck line, exquisitely Nautor, mediates the form of the hull. The market reacted positively, because the precious portfolio of loyal customers know that they can trust: every yacht bearing the name is always and in all cases a Swan.

In 1979 Ron Holland designed the Swan 371, slightly smaller (11.23 metres as against the 11.99 of the Swan 39). Holland's contribution to Nautor resulted in greater consideration for technological potential, aimed mainly at improving performance dynamics. Further design development would confirm optimisation of the length-volumes-performance relationship, the search for that special balance of all the elements of configuration that has always distinguished the essence of Swan and does even more so today.

In this context the Nautor management began collaboration with German Frers. Born to the trade, this designer took his first steps in his father's yacht design studio in Buenos Aires. Hired by S&S, from the two celebrated Stephens brothers he inherited that mark of extraordinary elegance to which he added, equally extraordinary, an inbuilt capacity for daring, for going beyond acquired canons. Frers knew how to interpret the Swan identity, that of the timeless object, over the course of a long collaboration that continues today.

Exemplary is the Swan 46 of 1983, 14.36 metres long. It opened a new avenue aimed at the flexibility of internal divisions, of rigs and equipment with view to satisfying owners' various requirements in a more multifaceted and customised way. It was

There's a way of going to sea that finds one of its most organic expressions in the "Spirit of Swan." A way that has been distilled over the years and transmutes the best of seafaring tradition into present day ways of organising free time and pleasure. Forty years of experience in the art of sailing, both racing and cruising, have outlined a highly characterised style of life, of thought and emotion that can act as an ideal reference in contemporary yachting.

There is a special relationship between yacht and helmsman, direct or indirect as it may be. From family cruise to ocean crossing, from races to regattas, the "Spirit of Swan" is personal involvement, deep and passionate, that links a man to his yacht so he can wholly experience sea and wind and enjoy them to the full. We shall try to follow some of its places and figures, following the thread[1] of its exclusive yet universal nature: a sort of screenplay-logbook, with its characters and adventures, and with the course and ports of call marked by buoys.

The Characters: Sea, Wind, Boat, Crew

The Sea

The great animal Earth, with a magnet for a heart, has on its surface an indefinable being, electric and phosphorescent, which is more sensitive, infinitely more fecund. Is this being, which is called Sea, a parasite of the great animal? No, it does not have a distinct and hostile personality. It fecundates, vivifies the earth with its vapours. It seems the Earth itself in that which it has of greater productiveness, in other words, its main organ of fecundity?

With the majesty of an ancient Germanic fantasy the sea comes up against us through the words of Jules Michelet who sang its

epic with the passionate optimism of a 19th century positivist. In the French historian's great fresco the sea is a living organism that has something of the animal: the tides are its pulse, its breath. In this sea as salty as blood, this sea which has a circulatory system, a heart and heartbeat, "there is a great number of delicate beings, more fragile than those on earth, which are cradled and suckled by its waters."[3]

Michelet's voice still echoes and vibrates under the most sceptical and disenchanted skin of modern yachtsmen. "This sea, in effect, does not generate mediocre passions. There is an indefinable electric beauty that one would wish to absorb entirely."[4]

It possesses what humans lack: superabundance, excessive strength, inexhaustible energy. Going to sea means absorbing this electrifying surplus. It means—in the words of Royal Yacht Squadron commodore John Grandy—"being a guest in the powerful environment of the ocean,"[5] experiencing dawns and sunsets, nature, freedom, adventure. Paraphrasing Steinbeck, sooner or later we realise that we do not put to sea but the sea puts itself inside us.[6]

First Buoy: Morphology of the Name
The word *sea* is feminine in some languages, masculine in others, and neuter in yet others. In French the sea (*la mer*) and mother (*la mère*) have the same phonetic identity. In Spanish *mar* has two genders: feminine for the good sea, origin of life, and masculine for the cruel sea that destroys and kills. Independently of the language spoken aboard and its grammatical habits, it is inevitable that any crew should sooner or later come up against not only the gentle, feminine and maternal wave but also the masculine violence of a heavy sea running, not to mention the boring and tedious neuter of a flat calm...

The Wind

He gave me a bag ...
stuffed full with the courses of all the blowing winds ...
He stowed it away in the hollow ship,
Tied fast with a silver string so there should be no wrong breath.
He sent me the Zephyrus,
To take the ship and ourselves ...[7]

A fair west wind drove Odysseus' craft as he left Aeolia, heading
towards longed-for Ithaca. Aeolus, king of winds, whose guest
Odysseus had been, had trapped his impetuous subjects in
a well-closed bag to ensure that the hero would make a tranquil
and fast passage. Believing the bag to be full of gold, Odysseus'
companions opened it and the unruly winds escaped... A storm
rose up, the destination once more fell into the distance and the
peregrinations of the "multifaceted and ingenious" leader were
destined to be further extended.
From myth to reality, the winds continue to blow or disappear
at their pleasure: with a sailyacht, "the only engine is the wind,
it challenges you every day," says Tom Stark,[8] Swan owner, ocean
sailor and racing enthusiast. Running on the wind or drifting
to leeward, clawing into it, tacking through it, interpreting its
excesses and refusals, stretching out on its bed... the seaman has
a kind of amorous relationship with the wind: he sniffs it, spies
on its dance, foresees its intentions, suffers its absence, bends it
to his will, entrusts himself to its arms, knows its tricks and fears
its furies.
To succeed in "using the elements to your advantage"[9] is
commodore John Grandy's strategy.
Apparently simple yet actually terribly complex, it seems to echo
the old Persian verse "I came like Water, and like Wind I go."[10]

The wind loves flexible and wise spirits, capable of leading the dance because they are part of the internal rhythm of the music: with a Swan playing first violin in the orchestra.

Second Buoy: Symbology of the Winds
A rose, symbolic flower par excellence, gathers the contentious winds in a figure that is harmonious and perfumed yet rich in thorns. Rose-wheel, corresponding to the compass rose, whose petals-spokes indicate the eight main wind directions.
There are a great many aspects of wind symbolism.
Together with the best known ones of vanity, instability and inconstancy, various traditions assign them important roles and meanings. In ancient Persia the wind was the support of the world and the regulator of cosmic and moral balances. In the Islamic tradition its numberless wings contain the water of the world. In the biblical tradition the wind is first of all the creating breath of God and the various winds are angel messengers of divine power. The druidic wind of the Celtic tradition could turn away invaders' ships, a manifestation of the druids' power over the elements. When it appears in a dream the wind announces an important event, a great change, and is the symbol of energy. In Ernst Aeppli's opinion it seems that "only oriental people can understand the meaning of the empty space, where the wind blows,"[11] but a good sailor always has a touch of oriental wisdom and great familiarity with that empty and mobile space.

The Boat
Carries out her work in perfect silence, with motionless grace, and appears to conceal a capricious and not always governable strength which takes nothing from the material reserves of the land. ... She seems rather to draw her strength from the very soul

Today, after forty years, there are third generation workers
and office staff at the Nautor premises. Some began as
students on work placement assignments during the summer
holidays and, once qualified, became fulltime employees.
The loyalty of the people who work there and who materially
create these thoroughbreds of the sea also contributes to
keeping brand value high and strong in a technological context
that is increasingly tough and competitive.
Why have your boat built by Nautor?
One of the many reasons is precisely the fact that you become
part of a circle of 2,000 owners who cross the seas to meet one
another, and of 500 people who build yachts with the highest
concentration of spirit, the "Spirit of Swan."
Roberto Franzoni

of interiors, the Finnish habit being to open premises where
the workforce is most concentrated. Unfortunately, during
the same year, the Edsevö yard was destroyed by fire. New
premises were already under construction when Edsevö burned
down and production was interrupted for only two months.
The company's majority shareholder was now the Schauman
Group, a Finnish leader in wood treatment. Nautor became
the group's Yacht Division. With a management more aware
of business exigencies and with constant perfecting of technical
constructional know-how, in the early 1970s Nautor could tackle
the implementation of decidedly important projects.
The highlight of this evolutionary phase was during 1972, with
the creation of the Swan 65. With an overall length of 19.68
metres, it was the biggest fibreglass yacht to date, available with
a ketch or sloop rig. The Swan 65 emphasised the perfect
integration of its contributors: Stephens design / Nautor's Swan
culture. A magical compendium of values, this object expresses
an excellence without precedent, a point of reference worldwide.
There are two twin cabins with bunk beds and access to a private
shower. The owner's cabin aft is comparable to an actual suite.
The external design crowns the evolutionary line of the great
racers of the period, resulting in an elegant vessel and a true
performer.
To complete the success in this series, Sayula II, with Mexican
owner Ramon Carlin at the helm, won the first Whitbread Round
the World Race (1973–74). It was an absolutely exceptional result
as the Swan 65 suffered no significant damage in spite of
capsizing in the icy waters of the southern latitudes. The Finnish
built hull was indestructible. Sayula II's victory was a clear
message, and the reputation of the splendid Nautor Swan yachts
grew on markets worldwide.

gained well deserved fame. In those days the use of fibreglass was certainly not a novelty, but Koskenkylä wanted a 10 metre yacht, a size that hadn't yet been experimented with. The Stephens' design for the Swan 36 was already in itself a harbinger of the new. The rudder was positioned fully aft, preceded by a skeg separated from the fin keel. The centre of the hull was shifted back and the application of a bustle, a swelling of the keel aft, gave greater steering stability.

The skill of technicians and workforce meant that Nautor could create a fibreglass vessel whose behaviour and safety equalled those of the wooden vessels of a glorious past. The living spaces could be better subdivided and the furnishings and fittings more comfortably arranged, thanks to the abilities of the yard's master carpenters.

If at that time it was still possible to compete at top level, at the helm of a fine "civilised racer," that first example of the 36 foot yacht highlighted the splendour of Swan yachts and their balance of form and tradition.

The Swan 36 immediately gained favour with owners. In 1968 David Johnson and Mike Hurrell, Nautor concessionaries in England, won all the Cowes Week trials in the second class with Casse Tete II. Agile and highly manoeuvrable, the Swan 36 came triumphantly up to the wildest expectations and production was speeded up as the yard grew. An attentive growth in which, right from the start, precision and organisation counted, in a place where ice and snow exert a vicelike grip for two thirds of the year. The success of that first model led to a demand for larger boats. Owners who had experienced the Swan 36 and others wishing to buy new yachts resulted in a customer portfolio of affectionate Nautor enthusiasts. In 1966 the Kronoby production premises went operational, dealing with carpentry and assembly

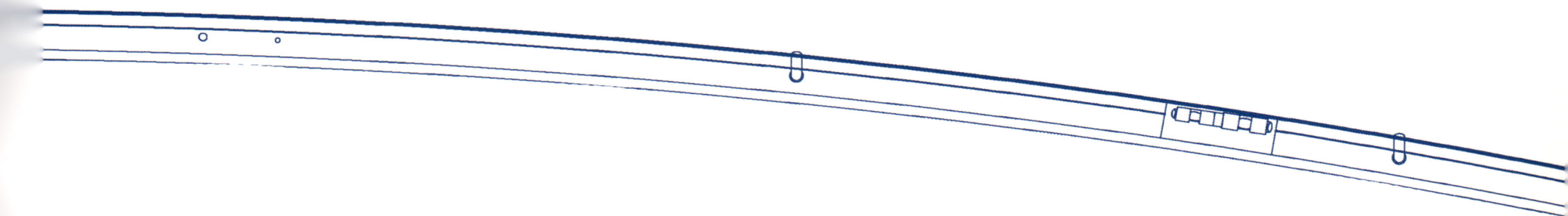

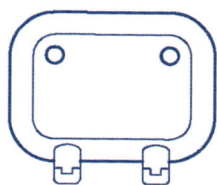

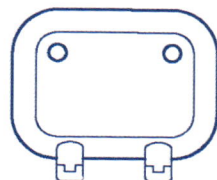

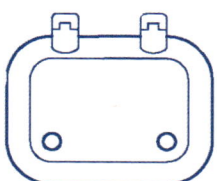

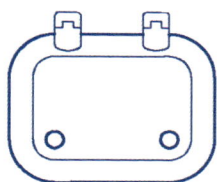

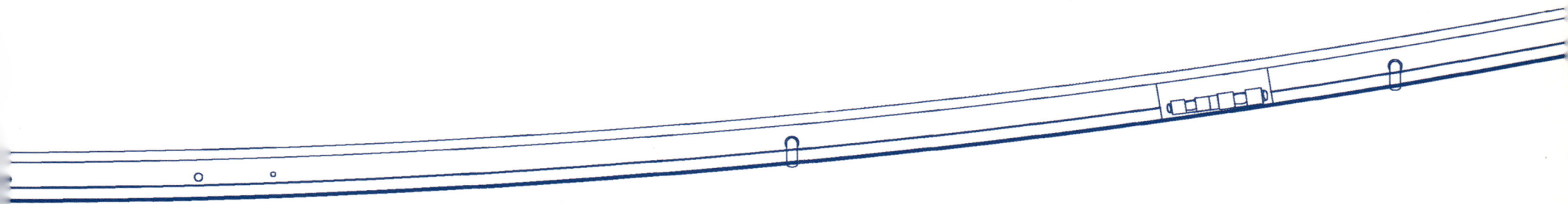

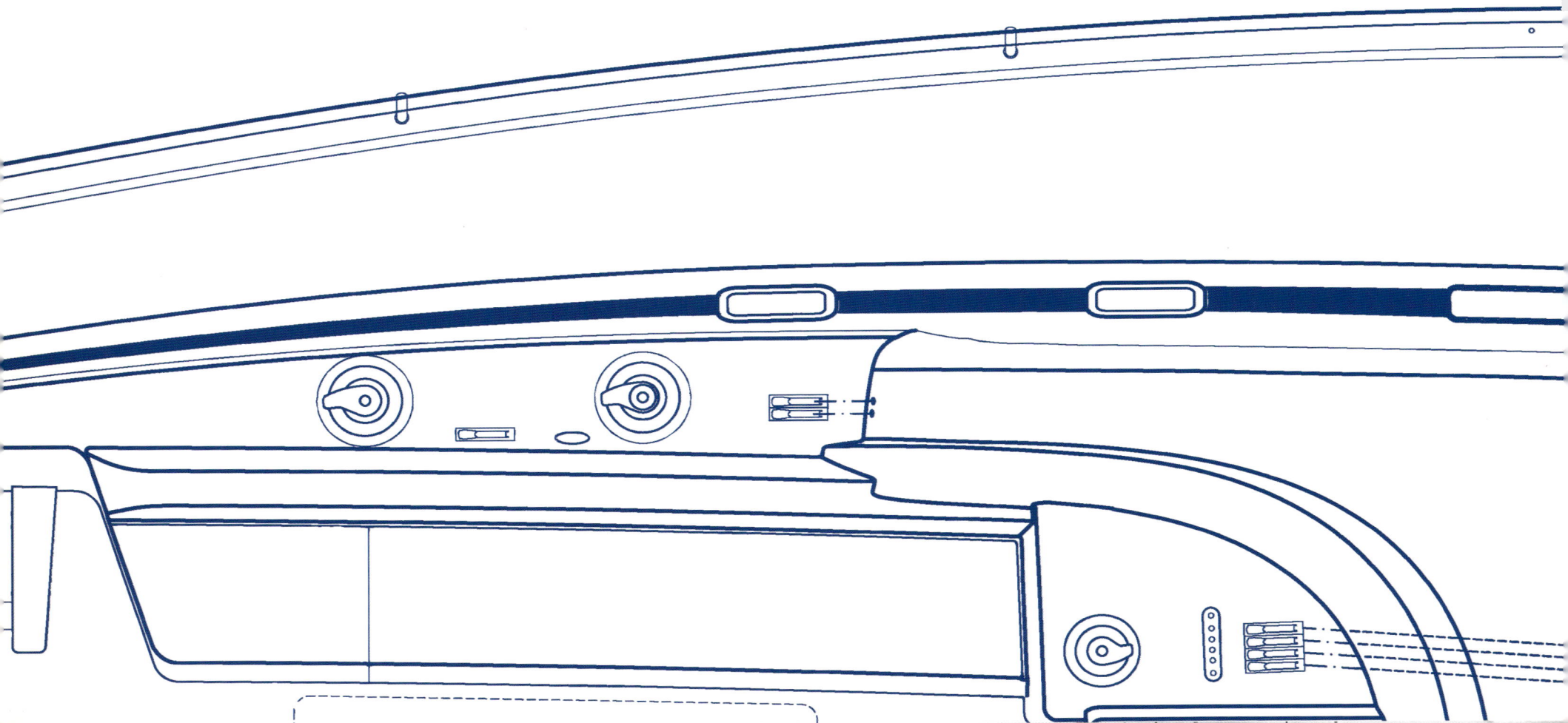

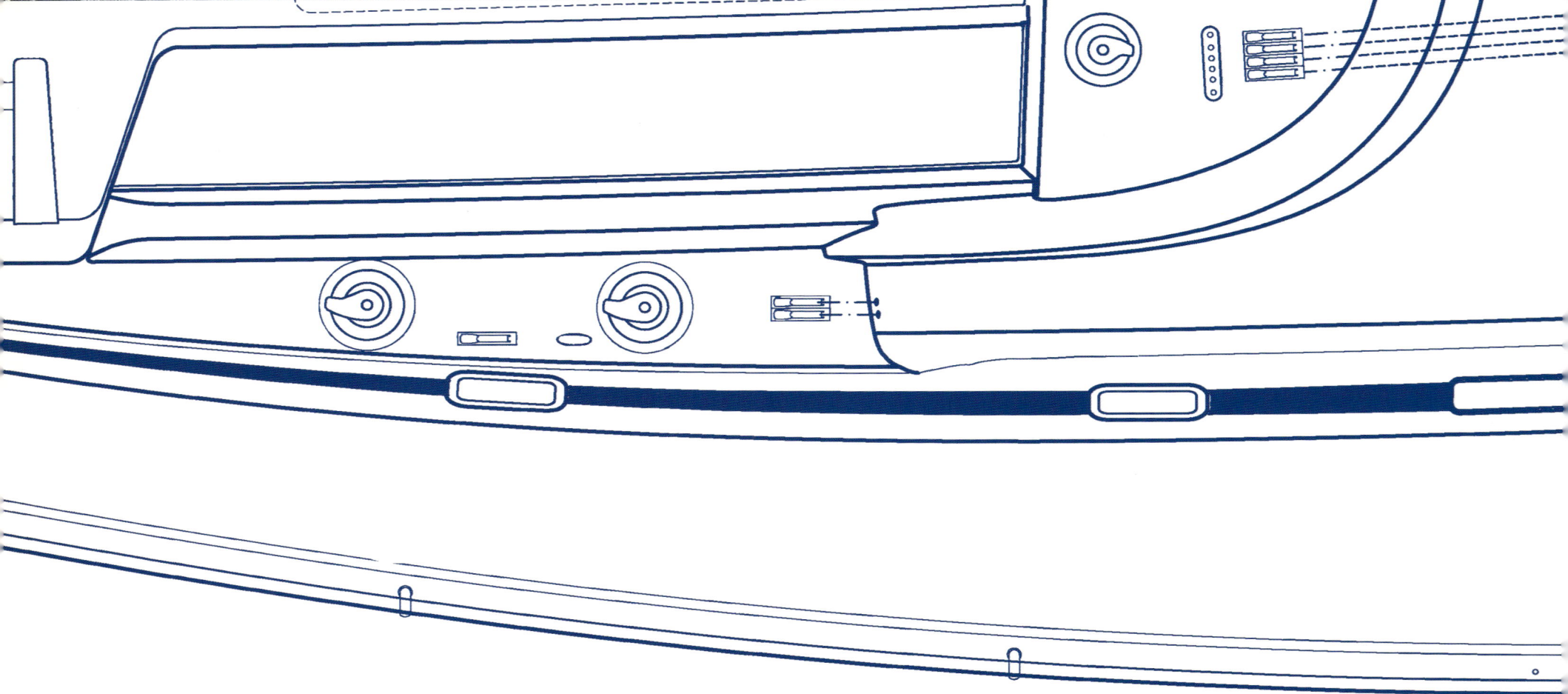

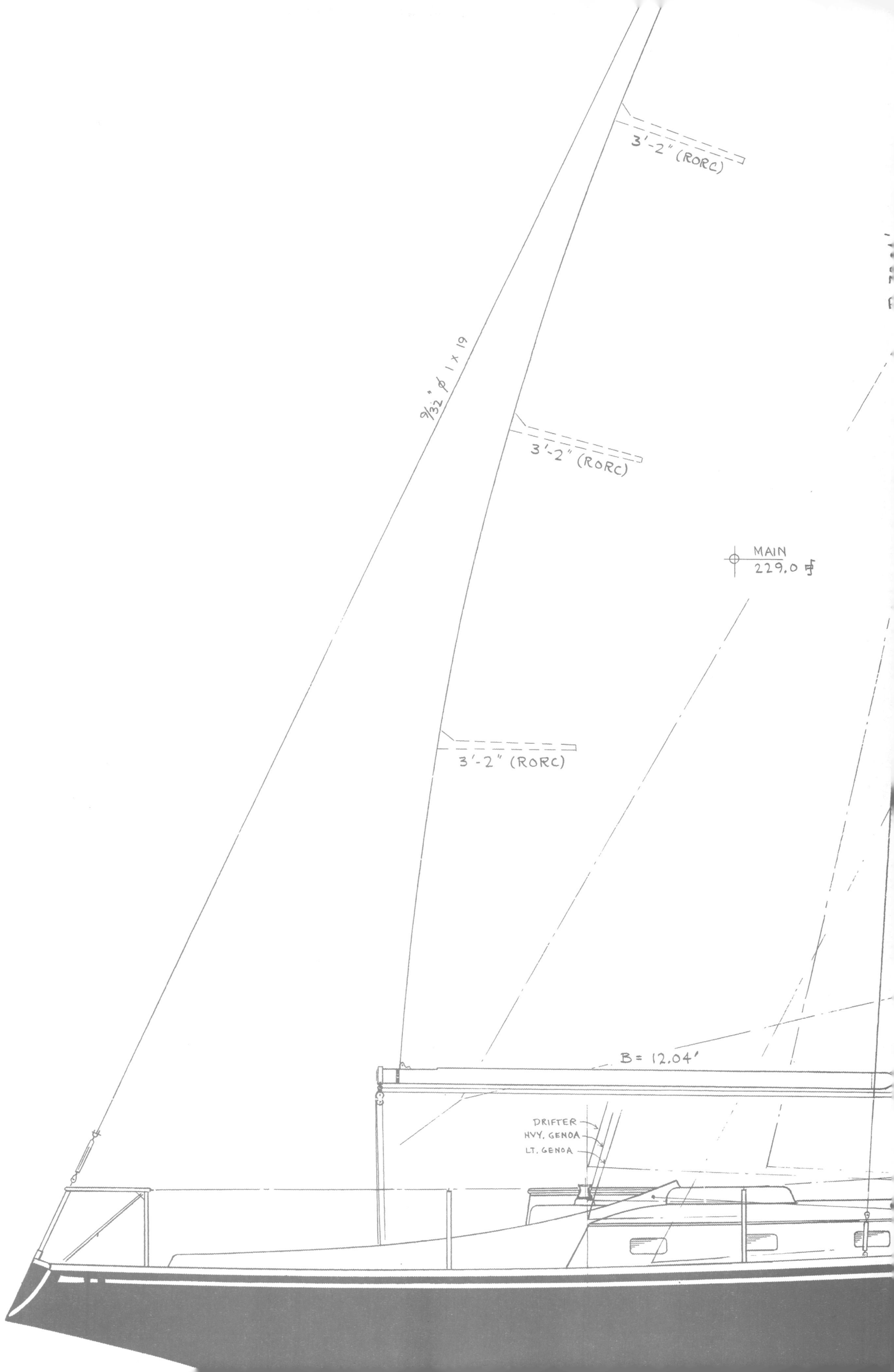

3'-2" (RORC)

9/32" Ø 1 x 19

3'-2" (RORC)

3'-2" (RORC)

MAIN
229.0 ⏥

B = 12.04'

DRIFTER
HVY. GENOA
LT. GENOA

TARAN:TELLA

felt had hardened in the glacial temperature and was difficult
to handle without breaking it.

Vatanen had to bring up buckets of boiling water and, standing
on the ridge, pour it over the strips of felt. The hot water thawed
the felt and Vatanen, working fast, could lay it out and nail it
firmly to the roof. It was a spectacle not to be missed: the hot
water steamed in the icy air, the roof was soaked by the steam
that rose high into a serene sky."

To the west, the pines and birches of magical Finland frame
the Gulf of Bothnia formed by the Baltic Sea. In the 15th century
the Finnish lidos were settled by their Swedish neighbours:
shipwrights, caulkers and other tradesmen, attracted by the
endless supply of timber. So the great tradition was established in
very remote times, with itinerant operational premises, in constant
research for top quality raw materials.

It was here that these fine craftsmen, by a process of slow
combustion, extracted pine resin and prepared vegetable tar for
caulking. The substance was even exported to Sweden, Norway
and other countries. With the same procedure they made charcoal
for the smiths' furnaces. Boatbuilding dates back to 15th and 16th
centuries. This explains why to this day there are still shipyards
along the arc of coastline and farther inland.

There is a curious parallel in other fields, first of all in home
and community furnishing. Finnish design was already well known
and appreciated before the mid 20th century. Alvar Aalto's work
is exemplary. Werner Blaser wrote in *Il Design di Alvar Aalto*
(Alvar Aalto's design): "The Finnish tradition is strongly linked to
the natural environment from which artists draw the bold forms
of their works. Nature is architecture. The labyrinthine model
of the many internal lakes, vestige of the primordial glaciers,
contrasts with the severe forests of pine and birch. Aalto's design

An ancient legend from the *Kalevala* (Finnish epic poems) believes Finland is a country of waterways and lakes where: "Everything was once all silence. The waters flowed, the winds blew, the waves broke on the shore but made no sound ... And the seasons went by almost with remorse because the joy that can make each day come alive said nothing. Everything was like a silent dream trapped on the threshold of sound. It was Väinamöinen, the magician that emerged from the ocean who, frightened by the solitude, began to play the harp ... And he was listened to by animals, plants, clouds, waters and wind.

So Väinamöinen ordered each to choose a favourite sound. The wind chose the reverberation of the magician's boots as he emerged from the ocean ... The waters preferred the sound made by Väinamöinen's long cloak whereas the trees found the rustle of his sleeves more melodious ... The birds found no sound that really pleased them except Väinamöinen's harp ... The fish were far less fortunate. They realised that something very important was happening but didn't know what. They could see the living things of earth and air opening and closing their mouths, but being under water the fish heard nothing. They decided to act like the others, but nothing happened. This is why fish today still open and close their mouths without emitting any sound."

In the far north the sun is the midnight sun, which for two months a year does not set and in winter, for the same period does not rise. Finland, or "Suomi" as the Finns call it, in the poetics of Arto Paasilinna is a land of woods and mysteries. In *The Year of the Hare* he tells of the predicaments of life in the tundra of Lapland. "Vatanen worked another couple of days on the roof, ... he removed the protection he'd built around the chimney, swept the snow from the roof and began to nail down the new bituminised felt to replace the old, which was worn out. But the bituminised

$5340 \, g/m^2$

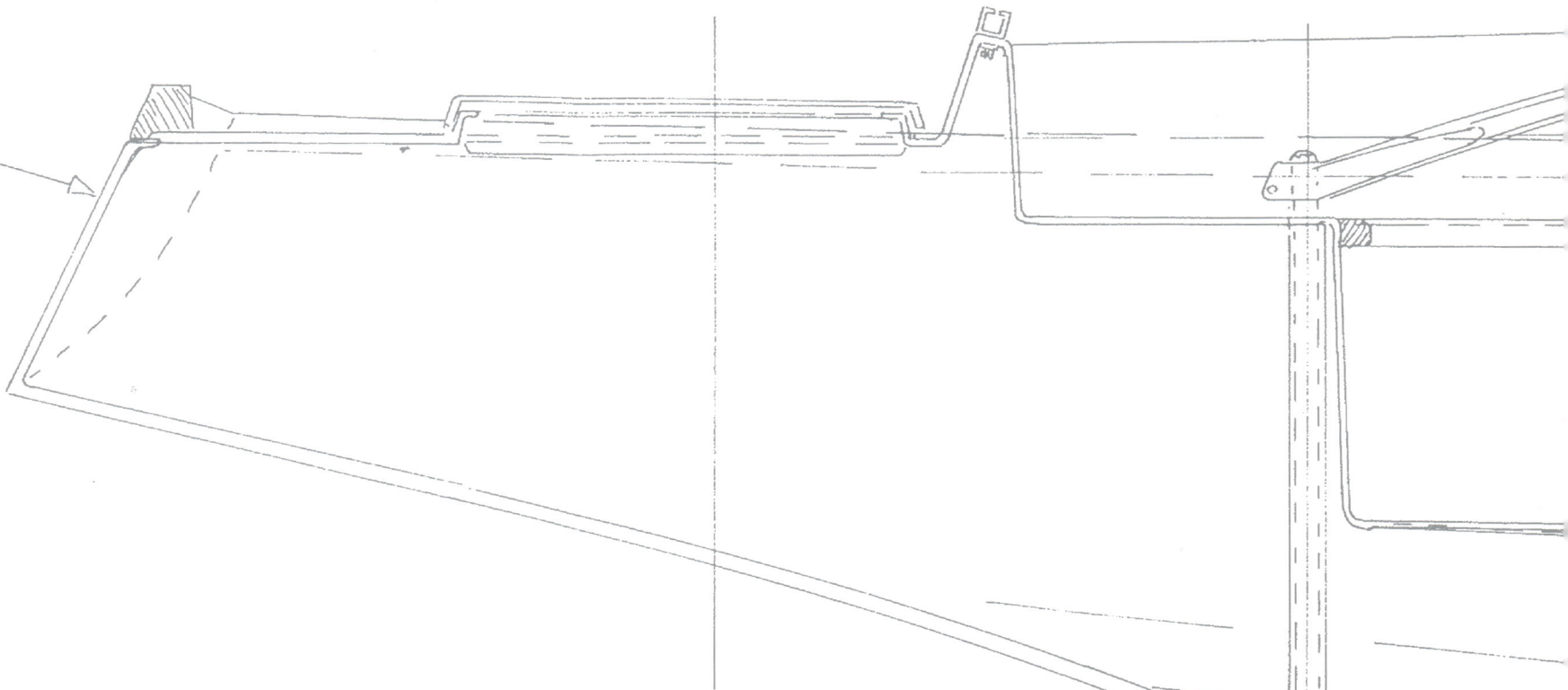

Stainless steel
6 mm

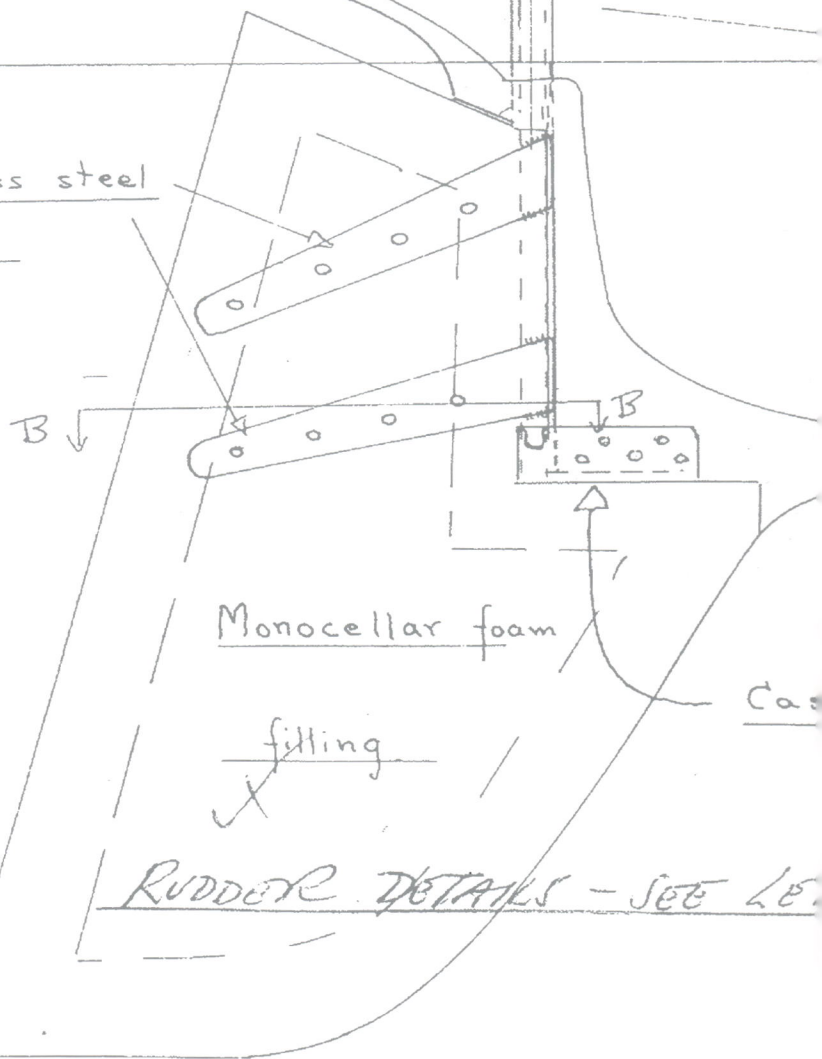

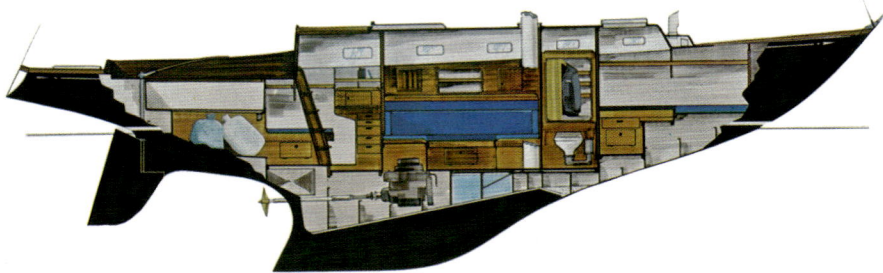

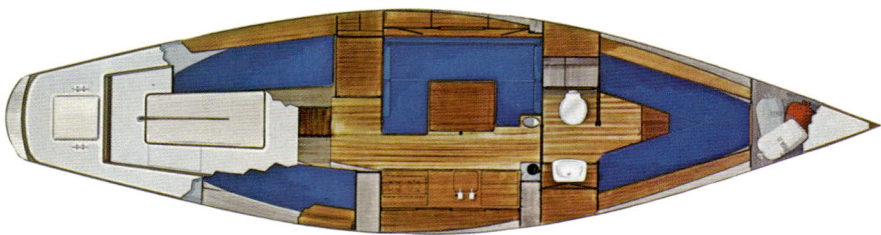

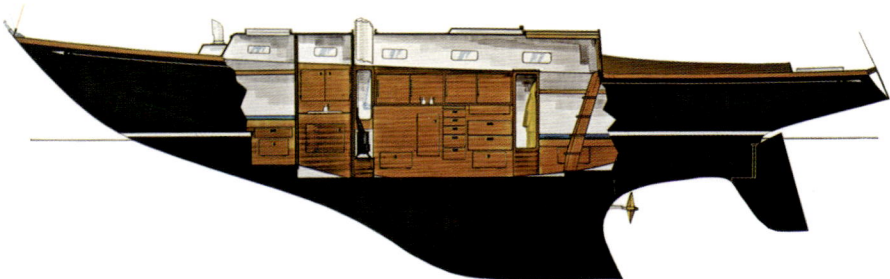

B

B

Monocellar foam

filling

RUDDER DETAILS - SEE LE

Cas

$\frac{3}{8}$

MAINSAIL AREA:
83.375 m²

TOTAL SAIL AREA:
175.175 m²

100%
91.80

P=23.000 m
I=25.500 m
IG=25.700 m

E=7.25 m

BACKSTAY NAVTEC ~30

RUNNERS Ø9 mm 1x9 WIRE

CHECKSTAY Ø6 mm 1x9 WIRE

BABYSTAY Ø10 mm 1x9 WIRE

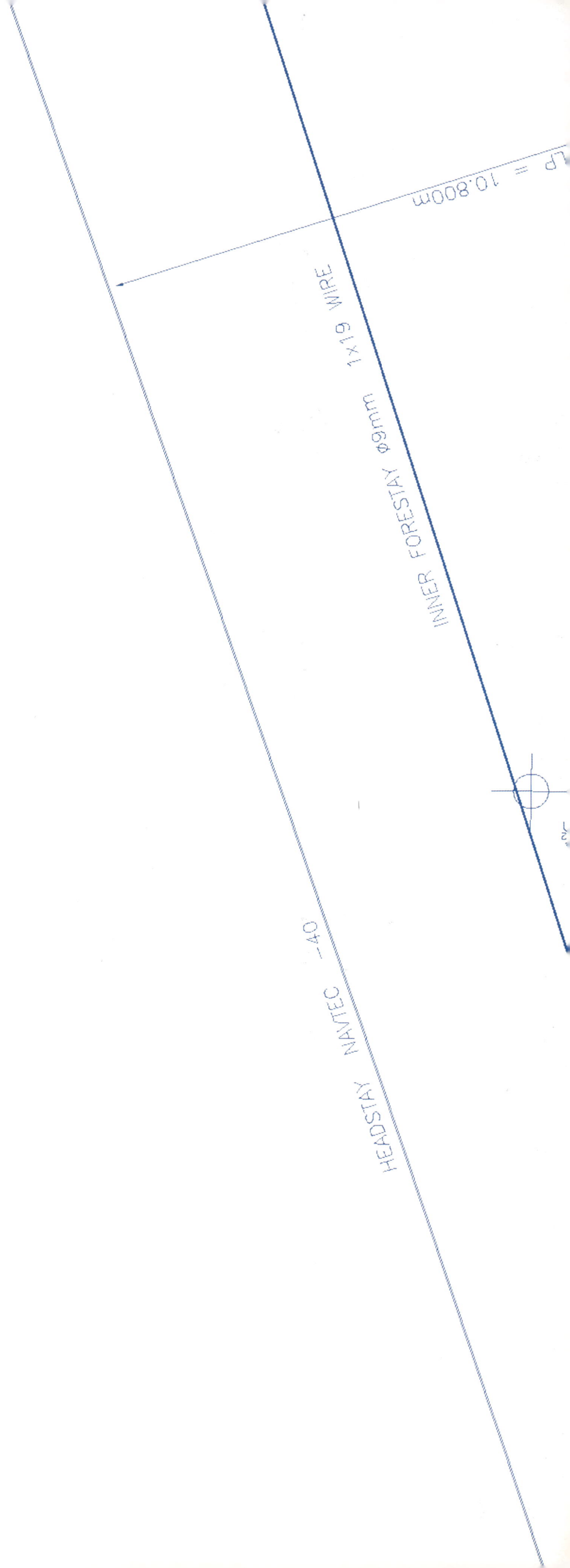

Photos

Swan 45 Class.

Swan 80, Favonius.

Swan 601.

ClubSwan

Rolex Swan Cup 2006.

Swan 45 Class.

Swan 80, Favonius.

Swan 601.

Swan 45.

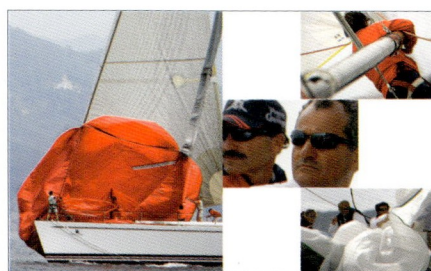

Zegna Trophy 2006. Rolex Swan Cup 2006; Paul Cayard and Leonardo Ferragamo; Rolex Swan Cup 2006.

Swan 100 FD, Fantasticaaa…

Swan 601, Cuordileone.

Swan 45 Class.

Swan 70, Manu. Pekka Koskenkylä; German Frers; Ron Holland, Olin Stephens.

Rolex Swan Cup 2006.

Swan 601, Spirit of Jethou. Swan 44, Aura; Swan 45, Wolf; Swan 112, Mistery; Swan 46, Ballytrim; Brenta 76, Silandra V; Swan 57, Matchless.

Swan Anniversary Regatta 2006, Turku, Finland.

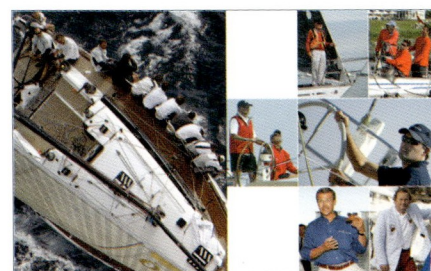

Swan 45, T…Too; HM Juan Carlos, King of Spain, ClubSwan Honorary Member; Russel Coutts, ClubSwan Guest Member; Swan Owners.

Swan 100 FD, Fantasticaaa…

Swan 45.

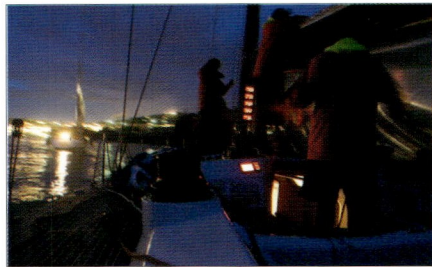
Back to the marina in Porto Cervo after the long race.

Aboard after the long race.

Porto Cervo, the dock.

Working after the race.

Relax.

Dock.

Sunset on the dock.

Yacht Club Costa Smeralda, Porto Cervo, Sardinia. Swan 45 Class Asprey Trophy.

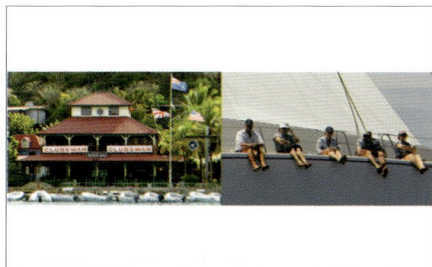
Bitter End Yacht Club, Virgin Gorda, British Virgin Islands. ClubSwan Caribbean Rendez-vous, British Virgin Islands.

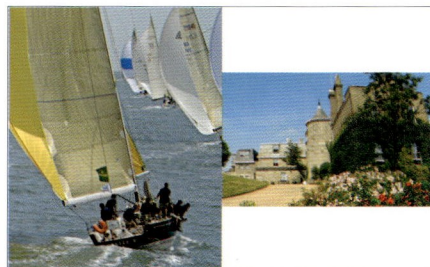
Rolex Swan European Regatta 2005. Royal Yacht Squadron, Cowes, Isle of Wight, UK.

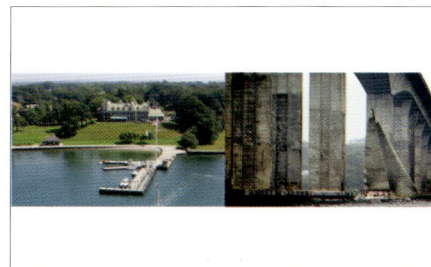
New York Yacht Club, Summer House, Newport, RI, USA. Swan American Regatta 2003.

Pricegivings.

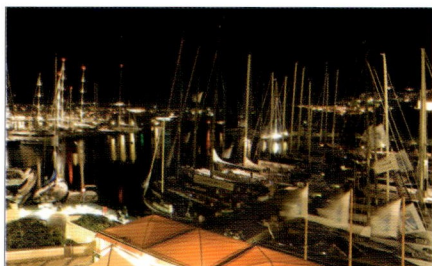
Porto Cervo Marina by night.

Party.

Anna aboard the Swan 100 S Hoppetosse.

ClubSwan Caribbean Rendez-vous, British Virgin Islands.

ClubSwan Caribbean Rendez-vous, British Virgin Islands; Claudio and Anna playing aboard.

Elena aboard the Swan 100 S Hoppetosse.

ClubSwan Caribbean Rendez-vous, British Virgin Islands.

Living the interiors. Margherita dancing aboard.

Cruising experience.

Relaxing aboard.

Watching the race.

Today

Swan 45 Class.

Swan 601, Artemis.

Swan 601, Spirit of Jethou and Artemis.

Club Swan 42.

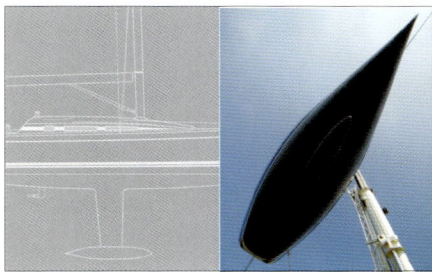
Club Swan 42.

Club Swan 42.

Swan 66.

Swan 46.

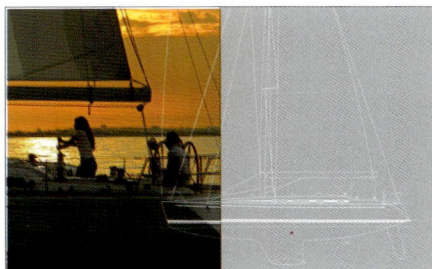
Swan 46.

Swan 53, Schatzi.

Swan 75 FD.

Swan 82 S, Nazca.

Swan 82 RS, Solleone.

Swan 82.

Swan 100 FD, Fantasticaaa…

Swan 100 S, Aquarius Alfa.

Swan 112.

Swan 112, Eratosthenes.

Swan 131, Aristarchos.

Swan 131, Aristarchos.

Swan 131, Aristarchos.

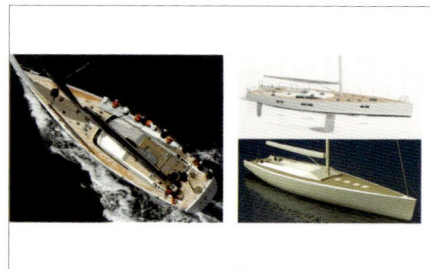

Brenta 76, Silandra V. Tripp 78;
Frers 82 (Lazzarini & Pickering).

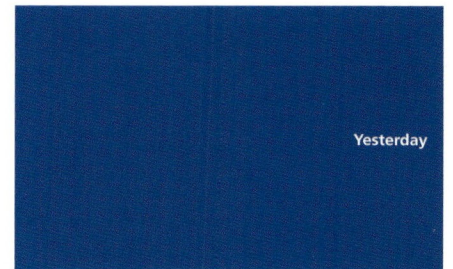

Yesterday

Swan 36, Tarantella, Sparkman & Stephens.

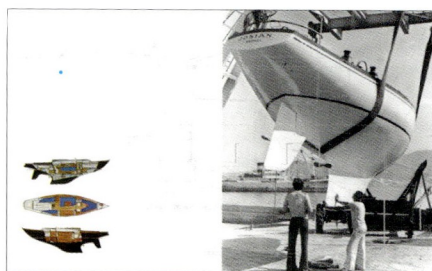

Swan 36, Josian, Sparkman & Stephens.

Swan 36, Tarantella, Sparkman & Stephens.

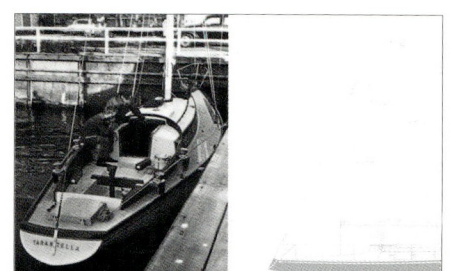

Swan 36, Tarantella, Sparkman & Stephens.

Swan 65, Blue Magic, Sparkman & Stephens.

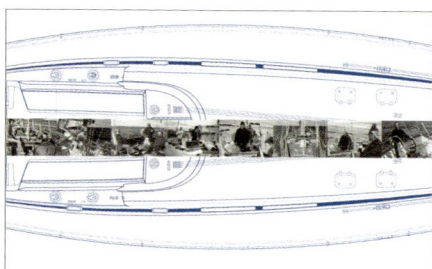

Aboard the Swan 65, Sparkman & Stephens.

Swan 65, King's Legend, Sparkman
& Stephens. Two photos of the Swan 65,
Sayula II, Sparkman & Stephens.

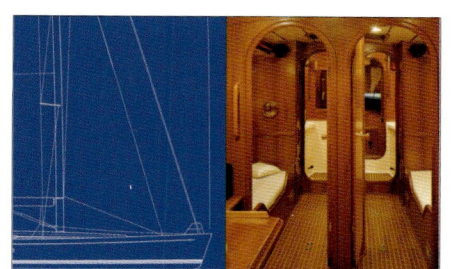

Swan 65 interiors, Sparkman & Stephens.

Swan 39 R, Black Swan, Ron Holland.

Swan 371, Lighea, Ron Holland.

Swan 46, Troubador, German Frers.

Swan 60, Orfeo, German Frers. Swan 60,
Orfeo, German Frers; Swan 60, Island Fling,
German Frers.

cover
Rolex Swan Cup 2006 (photo by Carlo Borlenghi)

texts
Decio Giulio Riccardo Carugati, Roberto Franzoni, Maria Sebregondi

graphic coordination
Dario Tagliabue

graphic layout
Anna Piccarreta

page layout
Chiara Fasoli

editorial coordination
Virginia Ponciroli

editing
Simona Oreglia

technical coordination
Mario Farè

quality control
Giancarlo Berti

translation
David Smith

photographs
Archivio Nautor
Kurt Arrigo
Matias Boettge
Carlo Borlenghi
Kevin S. Dailey
Francesco Ferri
Daniel Forster
Stefano Gattini
Luca Massari
Franco Pace
Paradisi & Borocci
Marc Pepper
Pertti Puranen
Patrick Roach
Mats Sandström
Erik Skallerup
Tim Wilkes
Tim Wright
Yacht Shots BVI Photography

www.nautorswan.com
www.electaweb.com

This volume was printed by Mondadori Electa S.p.A.,
at Mondadori Printing S.p.A. Verona in 2006